Who Has Got *Your* Back?

Inspiring You to Free Your Hidden Personal Power!

Christie Pinto

GOWOR
INTERNATIONAL PUBLISHING

Testimonials

"Christie is a flash of positivity and hope that cuts through the grey that contemporary society often projects. She has introduced me to a range of techniques that have helped me professionally, spiritually and mentally. Part coach, part mentor, part guru and mystic, Christie offers a holistic and personally tailored approach that has helped me become increasingly positive, productive, intuitive and able to navigate my way through life with a smile on my face."

Tin Hemingway, Music Maestro
www.tinhemingway.com

"Working with Christie as my coach over the years has helped me through stressful times at work by giving me a different perspective on the situation plus tools, tips and tricks to cope - which results in restoring faith in myself. Having known her when she worked in my industry, I already knew that she was intelligent, trustworthy and experienced in the world of business. What became apparent through our first coaching session is that she really cares and will put in all the effort needed for her sessions and more. I have always valued and continue to value her help and her ability to make me laugh no matter how seriously I am taking myself at the time."

Nina Genikis, Program Director

"I have known Christie for some 18 months now and in this time she has become a good friend and confidant. She is a good listener and doesn't reply with empty platitudes but makes valuable suggestion or asks questions to get to the crux of the matter. Her many strategies are useful tools to make everyday life run more smoothly and to provide balance in the long term. She provides a hands-on approach to a happier life."

Gerhard Moser, CEO
www.homeloanguru.com.au

"I have known Christie personally and professionally for 6+ years. I started talking to Christie professionally about 12 months ago, when I changed jobs and have achieved a deeper insight into myself as well as more positive and confident outlook on life and in particularly work. Christie has an intuitive insight into what is right (or necessary) for you at a particular moment in time, which is extremely valuable. Can't wait to see what is next."

Birgitte Thiesen Snelson, Procurement Manager

"Christie has been my coach/mentor for over a year now and has made a tremendous difference to my life. Her enthusiasm, passion and spirituality are truly inspirational. After reaping the benefits of working with Christie, I recommended her to my mother and daughter and they too have benefitted from her coaching. I admire her ability to work so effortlessly and patiently with different generations. Just by interacting with Christie, I aspire to be a better person as she leads by example. Thank you Christie for all the love, warmth and wisdom you shower on not just me but on my mother and daughter as well."

Sheree Cortes, IT Manager

"Christie has helped me work through all the struggles that were holding me back from achieving the very many goals I have. I found it's so important to have someone to keep you accountable for what you say you're going to do! Everyone needs someone to inspire them and help them develop skills to achieve more. You'll achieve even more than you first set out to do with a coach. Christie, you're a true inspiration and I love your work; thanks for all that you do!"

Angelo Castiglione, Strength and Conditioning Coach, Owner
www.180degrees.com.au

"I met Christie at a seminar during a very difficult period of my life, and we connected instantly. She has that bubbliness and joy for life that is hard to resist! So I began regular coaching sessions with her, and I always looked forward to them as my reward for a hard week… each session was a breath of fresh air, a blow of positive energy, a flow of sweet words in my ear, that would carry me lighter till the next session. She masters the art of making you feel good, of making you think differently, of transporting you in a new world where issues becomes opportunities, where pain becomes a door to strength, where conflicts become tools for learning new skills. She has helped me tremendously to overcome many of life's hurdles."

Dominique Delaisse, IT Consultant

"Christie has changed my life! Though I have many loving and well-meaning people in my life, their advice is often not the most suitable for my particular situation. Christie has taken me on a journey of self-discovery and ultimately self-love. At times when I was experiencing extremely high emotional discomfort, Christie provided me with tools and techniques that helped me move through not just the issue at hand, but they could also be applied to other areas of my life. I honestly don't think I could be in this place of happiness without Christie. To add to my experience of profound results, Christie is a delightful, energetic, loving, skilful, conscious human being whose commitment to your personal growth is unwavering."

Melanie Heskin, Burklyn Partner
www.burklyn.com.au

"If you are looking for someone to help you work through blocks in life or achieve goals, then Christie is the personal coach you want to have by your side. Her bright and energetic personality is infectious and you can't help but come away from each session with her feeling enthusiastic.

Christie has an innate ability to tune in with where you're at in the conversation. She is great at listening and uncovering what and where your blocks are. Best of all she is able to provide strategies you can take away and implement. Christie has considerable amount of years' experience in the coaching field. Most of all she walks the talk. You know that when she provides tips and techniques that she's lived it and experienced it. She's the real deal and working with her has certainly helped me to live the life I love!"

Tara Watson, Senior Consultant and Events Logistics Genie
www.activeconnectedcommunities.com.au

Who Has Got Your Back? Inspiring You to Free Your Hidden Personal Power
© Christie Pinto 2014

Crystal Clear Horizons www.crystalclearhorizons.biz

The moral rights of Christie Pinto to be identified as the author of this work have been asserted in accordance with the Copyright Act 1968

First published in Australia 2014 by Gowor International Publishing

www.goworinternationalpublishing.com

ISBN 978-0-9924977-1-2

Any opinions expressed in this work are exclusively those of the author and are not necessarily the views held or endorsed by Gowor International Publishing.

All rights reserved. No part of this publication may be reproduced or transmitted by any means, electronic, photocopying or otherwise, without prior written permission of the author.

Disclaimer

All the information, techniques, skills and concepts contained within this publication are of the nature of general comment only, and are not in any way recommended as individual advice. The intent is to offer a variety of information to provide a wider range of choices now and in the future, recognising that we all have widely diverse circumstances and viewpoints. Should any reader choose to make use of the information herein, this is their decision, and the author and publisher/s do not assume any responsibilities whatsoever under any conditions or circumstances. The author does not take responsibility for the business, financial, personal or other success, results or fulfilment upon the readers' decision to use this information. It is recommended that the reader obtain their own independent advice.

Dedicated to:

All the people in my life who have backed me at times when I could not and who have celebrated my successes with me when I could!

My wonderful brother Blaise who walked beside me on a difficult path for many years, and my dearest friend Martine, who is my biggest source of inspiration and support.

A Personal Note From The Publisher

Hi there!

As the Founder of Gowor International Publishing, my publishing company, I make it part of my practice to offer a personal review for each author about their book. The reason why I do this is so that YOU, as the reader, can glean a further understanding into why this book is so valuable to you in your life.

Very few individuals I have met in my life love coaching people as much as Christie. Over the time I have known and worked with Christie, I have been deeply moved by her continual devotion to awakening the human spirit within people who have, quite simply, forgotten that they have the real power to change their life for the better.

Who Has Got Your Back? is a beautifully written book that blends Christie's moving life story together with profound principles and teachings of healing and transformation that stand the test of time. Christie's every move in life is about making sure that people live fully – and this book reflects exactly that.

It has been (and is) a complete honour to publish *Who Has Got Your Back?* which I know is the first of many compelling and insightful books that the world will experience from Christie.

Enjoy the book!

With inspiration,

Emily Gowor

Founder of Gowor International Publishing

Contents

Foreword 1

Introduction 3

Chapter 1: Who Has Got Your Back? 7

Chapter 2: Losing My Backbone 21

Chapter 3: Backing my Dreams 35

Chapter 4: Backing a New Reality 57

Chapter 5: Back to the Past 83

Chapter 6: Backing Yourself By Taking Responsibility 99

Chapter 7: Back Your Own Happiness and Fulfilment 115

Chapter 8: You Have Everything You Need To Back Yourself ... 127

Chapter 9: Opposites: Back to Front, Front to Back 151

Chapter 10: Back to the Present 161

Chapter 11: Back to the Future 175

Chapter 12: Backing Yourself 185

Conclusion 195

Resources 198

Acknowledgments 199

About The Author 201

Foreword

'Back' on its own is an interesting word.

It has lots of meanings — '*back* to the future', 'my *back* hurts', 'he had his *back* against the wall' and two that I think are really pertinent here: 'coming *back* home' and 'giving *back*'. We'll explore those last two in a moment, but let's do what a foreword is supposed to do and focus for now on Christie's really interesting title for this great book: 'Who Has Got *Your* Back?'

There's a simple answer to that — Christie Pinto has.

That's because in this fascinating book, Christie involves you in her story in such a way that it becomes YOUR story — the story of how, just through thinking differently, we can change our outcomes. Or to put that in 'back' terms, we can change what we get *back* from living this life we lead.

Every chapter in this book (surprise, surprise) has the word 'back' in it. And every chapter takes you forward to an even better future. But it's not a future where Christie, or for that matter anyone else, is supporting you. As she points out early on in the book, 'The only person who can back you 100% of the time is YOU.'

And what Christie does so well, as she does each day for her personal coaching clients around the world, is to give you a powerful framework that becomes yours — one that has you getting your back. One that has you coming back home to living a life full of moments that matter.

The book goes even further than you think, too. And that's because for some time now, Christie has been a wonderful Lifetime Partner in the Global Giving Initiative, B1G1: Business for Good. Just by investing in this book, you're giving back — giving back in amazing ways to people who, most likely, you'll never ever meet. People who deeply appreciate the impact you're making.

You can see more about that by checking out Christie's details on B1G1: Business for Good right here:

https://www.b1g1.com/buy1give1/businessstory?companyID=780240.

Enjoy moving forward to discovering who's got your back. You'll love every moment of the journey.

Paul Dunn

Co-Founder and Chairman, **Buy1GIVE1 - B1G1®**

Introduction

"The most common way people give up their power is by thinking they don't have any."

Alice Walker

I wrote this book with the intention to pass on to you, my reader, some of the wonderful knowledge I have gained during my journey to heal both my back and my life. We are all born with this personal power, but it gets covered over by layers and layers of life events and mental conditioning. It is my deepest desire that you use what is contained within these pages to empower yourself in your own life, so that you can back *yourself* in all areas of your life as I learned to do. Through backing yourself, you will uncover this deep power within you to feel great about yourself and to create whatever you most desire.

My personal power lay buried within me for much of my life. For many years, I experienced severe stiffness in my back and my neck. Initially, I did not know what had caused it, but it affected the quality of my life. Sometimes, the stiffness was so severe that I felt like I was operating in a 'fog'. I found it hard to concentrate on reading or writing new material, which made my work even more of a challenge than usual. At other times, the stiffness in my neck caused me to feel dizzy as if I was drunk so that I could not drive. This meant that I had to rely on other people to drive me to wherever I needed to go.

The spine supports our entire body, and on a spiritual level, it represents how well you are coping with life, whether you are feeling supported and strong, or unsupported and helpless. In my childhood, I experienced severe challenges and trauma which led to me being very fearful of life. I grew up with the deep belief that I was simply not good enough. This meant that I often did not back myself, always looking to other people to support me or give me reassurance and validation because I could not do that for myself.

When this was not forthcoming, I would feel miserable and fall into bouts of fear and depression. This meant that although on the surface I was enjoying life in some ways and in certain moments, underneath there was a lot of internal suffering caused by self-doubt and lack of self-confidence. My emotions would go up and down like a yo-yo, driving me nearly insane, and I did not know how to make them stop. I longed to let go of my fears and feel balanced. I longed to feel fulfilled. I longed to have a sense of purpose. I longed to feel loved. I had momentary glimpses of feeling fulfilled, that I was on the right track in life and that I was loved throughout my life, but somehow they would then be snatched away by the lack of belief in myself.

My belief that I was not good enough and the self-doubt I experienced in my adult life meant that I would value the opinions of others above my own. I was often looking to other people for approval, and if I didn't get it, I would feel unloved. I would hesitate to make a decision for fear of making the wrong choice and would ask other people what they thought would be best. Throughout my career in software consulting, I was paid lower salaries than my colleagues, as I was too afraid to negotiate and ask for the going rate. In personal relationships, I put up with unwanted behaviour because I did not believe that I deserved better.

In recent years and through my self-healing journey, I discovered how the childhood experiences and the beliefs I formed about myself based on these experiences had affected my body. The way I had been dealing with life since my childhood had actually manifested into a physical form, causing a gradual deterioration and twisting of my spine. As I shared earlier, the spine is literally responsible for supporting us in life. If there are issues in the spine, it causes issues with our whole back and also the rest of our body. I finally discovered the root cause of the stiffness in my back and neck in recent years, which I share with you in the book.

Thankfully, I also discovered that you can heal yourself of anything. The first step is holding the belief that it is possible and then making a commitment to backing yourself in doing so. There is a strong connection between our mind and body. To heal the body, you also need to heal the mind and emotions. In recent years, I decided to back myself. I began exploring ways of healing myself both emotionally and physically. This has resulted in me freeing more of my personal power and has meant that I am now living a more fulfilled life than I ever thought possible.

This book is about backing yourself in life because no one else can. There are people who can assist you at times along the way, but in the end they also have their own lives to lead. The only person who can back you 100% of the time is YOU. I discovered this after many years of causing myself anguish to a degree that it actually started to affect me physically, leading to the deterioration of the vertebrae in my upper spine, twisting in my lower spine and the additional impact of these on my whole back and my neck.

Throughout our lives, some experiences lead us to form the belief that we are not able to back ourselves. We doubt ourselves. We judge ourselves. We put ourselves at the mercy of others. We subordinate ourselves to other people and social systems. We often feel that we can't rely on ourselves. Within this book, you will gain insight into how we are conditioned at an early age to believe that we are somehow not good enough and therefore do not trust and support ourselves in life. As stated earlier, our bodies and minds are very strongly connected, so our beliefs can manifest in our bodies as physical symptoms and pain as they did with me. All of this impacts us as adults and holds us back in life. This book is designed to trigger an understanding within you that you have everything you need inside you. In short, you can count on yourself, because you are amazing just as you are!

Although I share my personal journey with you and how my life experiences impacted my back, this book is not a biography. At times, some of the experiences I share with you are tough, but I am not looking for your sympathy or to shock you. The experiences I share with you in this book are designed to demonstrate that no matter what has happened in your life in the past and no matter what is happening in your life right now, you can move past it and even benefit from it as I did.

In writing this book, I seek to inspire you to use the principles it contains in order to empower your own life as they have empowered mine and also the lives of my coaching clients. To assist with this, there are exercises in all of the chapters. There are *Stirring It Up Exercises* to help you get in touch with what is happening within yourself. Then there are *Unleashing Exercises* at the end of the chapters that are designed to help you apply the principles in your life and trigger a shift in perception of yourself so you can see yourself more clearly. The intention is to help you free the personal power you have hidden within you! Furthermore, the intention is to inspire you to seek out additional principles and to look deeper inside yourself to see the awesomeness within so that you can truly live a life you love!

Chapter 1: Who Has Got Your Back?

"The only person you are destined to become is the person you decide to be."

Ralph Waldo Emerson

The theme of this book is about you backing yourself in life so that you can discover your own personal power. As you may have expected, the idea for the book arose from my own circumstances. For many years of my life, I felt unloved, uncared for, weak and helpless until I started to uncover the personal power that lay hidden within me and began to see what an amazing being I really am. My personal story serves as the backdrop to key principles which I am going to share with you. These principles helped me to empower myself and transformed my life beyond anything I could have imagined. It is my desire that they have as deep an impact on your life!

At this point, it is important to clarify the key themes that run throughout the book in order to set the scene for the following chapters. In this chapter, I am going to give my views on what 'having your back' means and also the significance and meaning of your back and spine within your life. You will undoubtedly have additional views and your own interpretation of both of these themes. Before going further into the book, you will also be given the opportunity to do an exercise to help you become aware to what extent you are currently backing yourself in life. At the end of the book, you will have the opportunity to revisit this exercise and review the impact that applying the principles within this book and doing the exercises contained within the chapters has had on you and your life.

What Does "Having Your Back" Mean?

There are many ways to interpret what 'having your back' means. What does 'having your back' mean to you? For me, there are two key meanings. One meaning is that you are being supported in some way, and the other is that you are being encouraged or promoted. The main thing is that when someone 'has your back', the person backing you will be encouraging you and cheering you on in your life. It is wonderful to experience this.

Starting with the first meaning, one type of support you may receive is when you are in trouble and there is someone there who helps you find a solution to the issue you are facing. This type of assistance makes it easier to quickly resolve the issue. Another type of support could be where you are being physically or verbally attacked and someone is right by your side and ready to defend you if necessary. He or she will not leave you by yourself, and will stick by you. They will be there to help you out until you are able to stand on your own two feet. Without this type of assistance, you would probably feel alone and helpless and have to work much harder to defend yourself and resolve the problem.

The second meaning of 'having your back' is when someone is promoting you or your ideas to other people, or that they are strongly encouraging you in your endeavours. They are cheering you on! There is someone who believes in you and is willing to demonstrate this belief to you or to others. It is always reassuring to have this type of backing. It means that you are not alone and it gives you a good feeling that there is someone who believes in you and is ready to assist you.

Something important to note here is that being supported means that you have someone you can *lean* on when necessary. However, you are still also doing things for yourself. It does not mean that someone is acting as a crutch for you, where they are the ones doing all the work to support you on a regular basis. If someone is acting as a crutch for you, they are propping you up, which takes away your strength and ability to help yourself. On the other hand, when you lean on someone occasionally, it strengthens you further because you are combining your capabilities and strength with theirs.

Take, for example, a situation where someone is often criticising you and there is a friend who defends you against these criticisms. Without this friend doing so, life would become unpleasant and you would probably feel under attack. However, if you continue to rely on your friend to defend you and do not do anything to put an end to these verbal attacks yourself, you are effectively letting your friend act as a crutch for you. In the long run, this will lower your self-esteem. You need to also speak up for yourself and find a way to put an end to the criticism. Have you found yourself in this type of situation?

Another example is your wanting a promotion or salary raise at work where you are reluctant to speak to your manager about it. A colleague feels you deserve the promotion or raise and speaks to your manager about you in glowing terms. In this situation, it is fine to lean on your colleague to start the process. However, if you continue to rely on your colleague to speak with your manager further, you are using him/her as a crutch. You also need to speak to your manager about your performance and capabilities yourself in order to get the promotion or raise. Can you relate to this?

So why is it important that you do not let other people prop you up? Of course, in the short term, it probably makes things easier for you. Unfortunately, in the long run, being propped up by other people can leave you feeling weak and powerless. You start to doubt yourself and it affects your self-esteem. In contrast, being assisted in doing things for yourself leaves you feeling stronger and more confident. It increases your self-trust and self-esteem. Additionally, it adds to the pleasure of life when you know that you are capable of supporting yourself, but that there is also someone you can call on to help you if needed. When someone has your back, it adds an extra dimension to your life of feeling both empowered and connected. It feels great to have someone who is a cheerleader for you!

But what if for some reason no one is available to back you? Well then, you need to be able to do it for yourself! Why do you want to be able to back yourself in life? Because it gives you the ability to create what you want in life. It puts the power of making your dreams come true firmly in your hands. It also sends out a signal that you are serious about your desires and becoming abundant and that you are ready for them to become a reality. What prevents us from backing ourselves in life? One of the key reasons is that we let our fears get in the way. The other reason is that we doubt whether we are capable of creating what we want. I explain the reasons for this later in Chapter 5. When someone supports and promotes you, it feels great. However, I know from personal experience that when you back yourself, it feels even better! The chapters in this book are designed to strengthen your ability to back yourself in life and, in doing so, free the personal power within you!

The Significance of the Back and Spine in Your Body

Many people have back problems at some point in their life. You may be one of them. As you are probably aware, on a purely physical level, your spine is part of your back and plays an extremely important role in your body as it is deeply connected to many essential functions. As this is not a book on human biology, I am going to give you a somewhat simplified picture of the spine and back in order set the scene for the rest of the book. I am also willing to admit that biology was never one of my strongest subjects at school, so simple works for me!

Your spine performs quite a number of functions in your body. These can be grouped into three key functions, which are:

1. Protect your spinal cord, the roots of the nerves in your body and some of your internal organs. The spinal cord is a column of millions of nerve fibres that carries messages from your brain to the rest of your body. If anything happens to interfere with these messages, your body will not function properly.

2. Provide support for the structure of your body and give you an upright posture. So any issues with your spine will affect the structure of your body and your posture.

3. Enable you to move flexibly. It provides support for sitting, standing, walking and other movements. Therefore, issues with your spine will impact the flexibility of your movements.

You are probably aware that there are several natural curves in your spine. These curves are important for helping you to stand upright and to have balance when you do. If any of these curves become too large or too small, it becomes difficult for you to stand up straight and affects your posture. Usually, you would take these curves for granted because everyone has them; they are just there and you do not usually need to pay any special attention to them. However, as soon as the curves change even slightly, you begin to notice the effect that it has on your body.

If for some reason you develop a twist or an extra curve in some part of your spine, it puts extra pressure on your vertebrae (the bones in your back) and the discs between the vertebrae. In turn, this pressure causes tension in the muscles of your back that are next to the affected area of the spine. The tension can lead to pain or stiffness or both in that particular area of your back. Additionally, if for some reason one or more of the vertebrae of your spine move out of position, it can create pressure on the nerves in your spine and irritate them. This causes interference with the signals or messages that travel over the nerves from your brain to your body parts such as your heart, lungs, stomach, liver and small intestines. Without receiving the messages, these parts of your body are prevented from operating efficiently; so, for example, you can experience heart problems, shortness of breath, ulcers, liver problems and digestion problems. These are just a few examples. Phew! That is how connected your body is! Yes, it is incredibly wonderful and pretty scary at the same time!

The discs between the vertebrae are made up of two parts: a tough outer part and a soft inner part, a bit like a jam doughnut. I hope that doesn't put you off doughnuts! The discs mainly act as shock absorbers between the vertebrae. Additionally, they hold the vertebrae together and allow for mobility in the spine. Issues with the discs can cause back pain, leg pain, neck pain and loss of flexibility in your spine. If, for example, the discs start to wear away, then the vertebrae are no longer as cushioned as they used to be and start to 'rub' together. Without the cushioning, your spine also becomes compacted and the vertebrae may start to fuse together; this affects the flexibility of the spine and restricts your movements, which can be very uncomfortable and very unpleasant.

When the types of disturbances described above occur, of course the quality of your life is often impacted. It can have an effect on your ability to work and play. Depending on the severity of the disturbances, you may even be impacted on a daily basis. For example, lack of flexibility in your spine makes it difficult to do sport such as jogging, tennis, gym work and dancing. Tension in your back and neck muscles disrupts the blood flow to your brain, which then affects your concentration and your ability to remember things. Moreover, constant back pain or discomfort can have a psychological impact on you, leading you to feeling depressed, anxious and irritable, or affecting your appetite and sleep. All of this can become so frustrating!

So now that I have described the incredible significance of your spine and back in your body, you are no doubt wondering how many of the above issues I have faced with my own spine and back. Quite a number as it goes.

Starting with my lower spine, I had twisting in the lower curve of my spine which put pressure on my vertebrae and the inter-vertebral discs. Although I did not experience pain, the pressure caused the muscles in my lower back to become stiff and uncomfortable. The vertebrae in my upper spine were deteriorating and some of the inter-vertebral discs had also worn away. Both of these factors caused pressure to be exerted on the muscles in my back and on other parts of my body such as my lungs. Additionally, I had scoliosis, which is when if you are looking at someone from the front, the spine is skewed to one side. This condition also caused additional pressure on my spine, the muscles of my back and other parts of my body. A few examples of the effects of scoliosis are shortness of breath, digestive problems, back pain or stiffness, fatigue and menstrual disturbances, all of which I experienced. I often had difficulty breathing fully, which made me feel tired easily.

My chest was often tight and I had difficulty breathing deeply. This resulted in my body being tense much of the time, and my thoughts never seemed to stop. Worse still, I had frightening dreams about not being able to wake up. In my dreams, I knew that if I could not open my eyes, I would die. When I tried to open my eyes, I found that I could not do it. This set my heart racing and scared me. I would keep trying to open my eyes without success, becoming more and more frightened all the time, eventually becoming terrified. When I became terrified, I would then, with a massive effort, finally open my eyes. I was alive! I lived another day! On the one hand, I was relieved, but on the other hand, my heart was racing at a million miles an hour and I dreaded having the dream again. A general practitioner (doctor) once told me that apparently lack of enough oxygen can make you hallucinate like this at night. This disturbance to my sleep of course added to my feelings of tiredness, although fortunately it did not happen on a regular basis, otherwise I would never have been able to get out of bed!

The issues with my spine also impacted my digestive system, which did not always work properly. I often felt bloated and uncomfortable, despite the fact that I was eating a healthy diet. The bloating also resulted in my clothes being tight around the waistline, which was unpleasant. I admit that my vanity did not particularly like this either! As you will have gathered, I spent a large part of my life in physical discomfort.

Due to my back muscles and neck muscles being constantly stiff from the condition of my spine, the blood did not flow properly to my head. Additionally, one of the vertebrae in my neck was sticking out more than it should. I was often asked by therapists if this was from an accident, but I could not recall anything happening that would cause it. The position of this vertebra caused extra stiffness and discomfort in my neck. This caused me to feel dizzy and nauseous at times, and at other times, my concentration was pretty poor. These symptoms scared me. Sometimes I was afraid that my body was shutting down and that I would either end up immobile or would die an early death. Either scenario was deeply distressing. As you can imagine, the symptoms I have described caused me to be on an emotional see-saw. One moment I'd feel pretty depressed, then later on I would be pretty irritated and frustrated. Of course this meant I did not feel particularly strong and in control of my life, which then led me to feeling disempowered and unhappy. It was definitely not a helpful state to be in, and greatly impacted the quality of my life. That is, of course, until I found out about what was causing the issues in my spine and back.

The Mind-body Connection

It's likely that somewhere along the journey of your life you have heard that there is a strong connection between your body and your mind, but what does it mean? It means that your thoughts, emotions, beliefs, decisions and attitudes can affect the way your body functions. When you have a thought, your body reacts immediately to that thought. For example, if you have thoughts about how much you have to do for the day, your heart will beat faster, your muscles will contract and your breath will move up into your chest to get you ready for taking action!

I did not know about the presence or significance of the mind-body connection and that I could help myself by changing my thoughts or my breath until about ten years ago. For example, my mind was constantly churning, which used to drive me crazy! I found that by changing my thoughts or my breath, I stop this 'mind churn' from happening. So what happens if you have thoughts such as 'Life is great'? Your body will produce chemicals such as endorphins, giving you a natural lift and causing you to feel good and even energised. Thoughts such as 'Life is hard' will produce a different mix of chemicals in your body, causing you to lose energy, feel tired and even slightly depressed.

From this, it is clear that what is going on in your mind can affect your body in a positive, beneficial way or a negative, detrimental way. This then has a tremendous impact on how healthy your body is overall. Additionally, what you eat and drink, how much you exercise and how well you look after your body overall will also affect your mind. If, for example, you drink too little water, your body will become dehydrated, your energy levels will be reduced and your thoughts are likely to tend towards the negative. And now for the good news! The great part about this mind-body connection is that it means you can use your thoughts to influence your body to better health and use your body to influence your mind to have more positive thoughts. The key is to always be aware of this connection and use it to your advantage to create an overall sense of well-being.

The Meaning of the Back and Spine in Your Body

So what is the meaning of the spine and back in the context of your life? On a spiritual level, the spine and back represent the level of support you have in life or, rather, the level of support you *perceive* you have in your life. I will explain what I mean by 'spiritual' a little later on when we reach Chapter 2. The back and spine also represent your alignment with life. A curved spine, or one with 'kinks' in it, such as when you have scoliosis, represents a misalignment with life, which means that you are not going with the flow of life. Instead, you are experiencing fear and not trusting life. Issues with different parts of the back are believed to represent various issues with life.

In her book *You Can Heal Your Life*, Louise Hay writes about the connection between your body and the underlying life issues and emotional issues you have been facing. Regarding the back and neck she writes that:

- The lower back is associated with 'Fear of money' and 'Lack of financial support.'

- The middle of the back with 'Guilt' and being 'Stuck in all that stuff back there.'
- The upper back with 'Lack of emotional support. Feeling unloved. Holding back love.'
- The neck 'Represents flexibility. The ability to see what's back there.'

I only discovered the book around February 2008 after having had the issues with my back for most of my life. When I read what Louise had written about the body and how it was impacted by life and emotional issues, I was stunned. Up until that point, I'd had no idea of the mind-body connection I wrote about earlier. Prior to that, no one had explained to me so clearly the impact that the earlier part of my life had on my back. I had indeed experienced all of what Louise wrote about in my earlier life. I felt as if she had written the book especially for me!

As a child and throughout the young adult and adult years of my life, I had indeed experienced money worries and lack of financial support, which is linked to the twisting of my lower spine. You may recall that I also have scoliosis of the spine, which comes from my having often felt fearful in my life and feeling as if I was not in the flow of life. The deterioration of the vertebrae in my upper spine comes from my not feeling loved or emotionally supported through much of my life. When you feel like you are not loved or supported, you become fearful, and that can make you feel as if no one has your back. Worst of all, you do not have your own back. Fear can also cause you to be less flexible, as you need to try and control everything in order to keep yourself safe. Later in the book, I will cover the history of how this fear came about.

As well as the structural condition of my spine causing tension in my back and neck, there was an additional source which added to my discomfort. Earlier, I wrote about the incredible connection between your thoughts, emotions and body: the mind-body connection. Due to this connection, your thoughts and emotions can create tension in your body, which then leads to physical conditions or ailments. In my case, the tension impacted my back further, but you may find that tension caused by your thoughts has shown up in other ways in your own body, such as severe headaches, stomach ulcers and heart conditions. So although I described the physical condition of my spine and back earlier in the chapter, the underlying cause for the condition was indeed my life experiences and my reaction to them.

The Impact of Not Backing Yourself in Life

When you do not back yourself in life, you have no sense of personal power. You are prone to self-doubt, self-judgement and fear. You feel as if life happens to you rather than you being in charge of your own destiny. As a result you can become anxious about your future because you do not know what is 'around the corner', so you spend time and energy worrying about it. When you do have your own back, you are ready to accept whatever comes in life because you know you will be able to deal with it. One of my coaching clients found himself in a situation where he had to back himself and found that doing so brought him some amazing results.

My client is a successful photographer. In his industry, the work is subject to a great deal of fluctuation throughout the year, where one month he can earn nothing, and in another, he may earn thousands of dollars. When he first came to me for coaching, his biggest concern was that he had reached a quiet period in his professional work. This was causing him some anxiety about whether he would be able to pay his bills (i.e., the mortgage) and provide his family with a certain level of lifestyle. As I listened to him describe what was happening in his life, I quickly realised that he did not have his own back. In spite of the great success that he'd had to date in his field, he still doubted his own abilities. I asked him how many times in the last ten years he had not been able to find work. Upon reflection, he realised that there had been only one time two years ago that he had been unable to find photography work and since then, he had always managed to find photographic projects.

We did some work together to help him connect with the fact that he is a talented photographer who has received great feedback for his work to date and has even won awards. I also gave him some ideas of how he could go about finding new clients for himself. He started backing himself and instead of sitting at home worrying, he became more proactive in creating opportunities for himself. He started contacting clients and agencies and started romancing them by taking them out and being in touch with them regularly.

As a result, he found that some clients who had put their projects on hold contacted him and offered him the work as soon as they got the go-ahead for the projects. Other clients started engaging him for well-paid assignments and then engaging him for further assignments. The money he generated from the work enabled he and his family to move into a new home. At a time when other people he knew in his industry were not getting much work, he was! This is a great example of what happens when you start to back yourself in life.

So, how about you? Before you read the rest of the book, now would be a good point at which to check in with yourself. How much do you back yourself in life? Below is an exercise to help you find out!

Stirring It Up Exercise: How Strongly Have You Got Your Back?

The following exercise is intended to help you get a feel for how much you back yourself in life. It is not an assessment that will give you some sort of rating. The scores are intended to help you become aware of how strongly you back yourself and also to highlight where there is room for improvement. The exercise is divided into two parts: Part A and Part B. It is intended solely for you; no one else has to see your answers. So I suggest that you put aside any feelings of shame or guilt about any of your answers and you will enjoy the exercise even more!

Part A

Below are a number of statements which relate to not having your own back. The purpose here is to give you an insight into the different ways it occurs which you may not have been aware of previously. Read through the following fifteen statements and answer "Yes" or "No" to each one of them.

- I have a good deal of negative self-talk going on in my head.
- I do not congratulate myself on finishing tasks.
- I feel uncomfortable when people pay me compliments.
- If something in my life does not go the way I want, I beat myself up over it.
- I find it hard to sit down for more than five minutes without feeling agitated.
- I need everyone to love me.
- I feel like an imposter who will get found out.
- I feel I lack the skills necessary for success.

- I obtain the opinion of others before taking action.
- I doubt my ability to make decisions.
- I make a decision and then change my mind.
- I delay making decisions in case I make the wrong one.
- I take action and then regret it.
- I often feel like I am not doing enough in life.
- Life is OK.

How many of the above statements did you answer "Yes" to? The more you answer "Yes" to, the less strongly you have your own back. There is no need to feel bad if you answered "Yes" to any of the statements, as it just shows you that there are some areas that could be stronger. Some years ago, I would have answered "Yes" to nearly all of them!

Part B

Here are a number of statements which relate to having your own back. The purpose here is to give you an insight into the different ways that indicate you have your own back which you may not have been aware of previously. Read through the following fifteen statements and answer "Yes" or "No" to each one of them.

- I know I can rely on myself.
- I congratulate myself on finishing tasks.
- I am kind to myself when I make a 'mistake'.
- I forgive myself for being human!
- I listen to the opinions of others and then make up my own mind.
- I accept that I have 'negative' traits as much as I do 'positive' traits.
- I give myself permission to relax and recharge my 'battery'.
- I do not expect everyone in the world to love me.
- I know that on some days being grumpy or feeling down is the best I can do.
- I take the pressure off myself whenever I feel overwhelmed.

- I trust myself to make a decision and then act on it.
- I stick with my decisions and follow them through.
- I have an optimistic outlook on life.
- I feel like I am my own best friend.
- Life is great!

How many of the above statements did you answer "Yes" to? The more you answer "Yes" to, the more strongly you have your own back. I can answer "Yes" to nearly all of these, which shows me I have come a long way in backing myself in life! You have probably noted that I said "nearly" because backing yourself is an ongoing process and there is always room for improvement and further growth. Backing yourself in life is extremely important if you wish to make the most of your time on this planet. Your reward for not doing so is that you do not feel fully alive, you feel like something is missing and find yourself wondering 'Where did all that time go and how did I get to my current situation in life?'

For much of my life I did not feel as if I was living life to the full. On the surface, I seemed to be 'really living', but underneath, I experienced a lot of pain until I discovered the power hidden within me. A power which exists in all of us.

Who Has Got *Your* Back?

Chapter 2: Losing My Backbone

"Have faith. Every event we experience and every person we meet has been put in our path for a reason."

Cheryl Richardson

At times an unexpected event occurs or we have an unexpected realisation that turns our world upside down. Maybe we discover that we have a health condition that we had not known about before and we start to become worried or even anxious about it. Perhaps we lose our job or our business and we are shocked and disempowered. Maybe we realise that someone in our life has kept something hidden from us until now and we are deeply disappointed when we find out. Perhaps someone has been behaving strangely and now we find out why and become angry with that person. Our reaction to the event or realisation from that moment on shapes our future and changes the course of our destiny.

When we first make an unexpected discovery, our mind spins and we often don't know what to think in this situation because it is a shock to our system. When we are unable to think clearly, we are uncertain as to how we should respond. Then, as the shock lessens and the realisation settles in, we start to react. This reaction could be a deliberate, considered course of action which helps us to move forward in our life in a positive way and turn our world the right way up again, or it can be a knee-jerk reaction which is not properly thought out and then creates more pain for us, leaving our world in chaos. For example, we may find out the reason behind our partner's strange behaviour and realise that there is an issue in our relationship. If we decide to respond in a considered way and work with our partner to try to find a resolution to the issue, it will restore harmony. In contrast, if we immediately get upset and shout at them or even decide to break up with them, it will put our life in turmoil.

Our response depends on what our level of awareness or spirituality is. When I speak about spirituality, I am not referring to religion. Spirituality is sometimes defined as "relating to or affecting the human spirit or soul as opposed to material or physical things." According to Wikipedia, in modern times, "social scientists have defined spirituality as the search for the sacred," and "connotes a blend of humanistic psychology with mystical and esoteric traditions and eastern religions aimed at personal well-being and personal development." Whew! Now for the plain English versions!

There are a multitude of definitions people use, which include a belief in the existence of a higher power that is greater than the individual, a sense of interconnectedness between all living things, a connection between all things living and inanimate and an awareness of values, purpose and meaning in life. To me, spirituality encompasses all of these things. For me personally, spirituality means you have a belief that there is a power or an energy operating in the universe that is greater than any individual. Some religions refer to this power as God and perceive it as a higher being, and people who do not follow an organised religion refer to it as the Grand Ordered Design or energy which creates and coordinates everything. Spirituality is also about you having a sense of purpose in life, the beliefs that you have around the meaning of life and your sense of connectedness to yourself, to others, to nature and to everything that exists. What does spirituality mean for you?

Spirituality is often connected with religion, but I know many people who live a spiritual life where they are aware of the connection between everything that exists and seek to live a purposeful life which honours their values, but they do not follow an organised religion. I am one of those people. Your spiritual beliefs have a big impact on how you respond to the expected events in your life that I referred to earlier. My personal story illustrates this.

My Back Gets in the Way

In 2001, after living in London for the majority of my life, I moved to Berlin to live with my then-boyfriend, Eiko. I was leaving behind my support network of my younger brother Blaise and my close friends. I had never done this before.

Chapter 2: Losing My Backbone

My friends were both shocked and excited for me. They asked me questions, which made me feel uncomfortable: "But isn't it going to be risky? You are so well set up here, your career is thriving, you have all your friends and your brother is here. Do you really want to just throw it all away?" These questions were understandable. Yes, it was risky and I felt very nervous about taking such a big step forward. I felt doubts arising about my decision. The old fear I had about taking any major step forward reared its ugly head. However, I certainly did not feel like I was throwing anything away. Something inside me just knew it was time for a move.

I had lived in London for twenty-seven years, since the age of seven, and I had experienced so much there, but I had a feeling deep inside of me that new adventures awaited me. In the previous years, every time I had gone away on holiday, I had sensed a longing within me to experience living somewhere else, but had not done anything about it until I went to Australia in 1996. After a holiday there, I just knew I wanted to move there for a while. However, Eiko wanted to finish off his studies, so we decided to live in Berlin and to delay the move to Australia for a few years. So in spite of my nervousness, I packed up everything and off I went to a new life in Germany. At this point, I noticed some sadness at leaving and at the same time, a sense of determination. However, I was so ready for this. Have you experienced something similar in your life where you did something even though you were nervous about it?

Berlin is a city like no other. It is exciting, vibrant and also has a certain edge to it, which makes living there very interesting. After a few months living in Berlin, I felt very happy about having made the move and my nervousness soon became a distant memory. Looking back now, I realise that if I had let my fear of the unknown get the better of me or taken on board the fears of my friends, I would not have experienced living in such an amazing city and been set on the path that I am on now.

Before moving to Berlin, I had the good fortune to be offered an exciting role specialising in the area of supply chain planning. As I was a member of a pan-European team, my manager lived in Vienna and I had the freedom to live anywhere I wanted. At that time I had been doing this type of work for twelve years, so my skills were sought after. I loved it! Sure, there were some long hours, stress and pressure, but I accepted these as being standard in the industry. On the other hand, the rewards were great; I got to travel, which is one of my passions in life, and I got to create solutions to problems, which is another of my passions in life.

Every week I would fly from Berlin to Frankfurt and regularly to other beautiful European cities to meet with other members of the team or clients. The members of the team were great to work with and we had a supportive manager who did his best to make our lives easier. Best of all, I got paid really well for doing things I loved! On the outside, life really seemed to have taken a turn for the positive.

However, there were two major aspects of life that were not so great. The first was my constant fear of something going wrong. No matter how positive things seemed to be, I always had a feeling that it would not last, that I could not allow myself to become too happy, because then it would all be taken away from me. I will cover this theme in more detail later in this book. The second aspect that made life more challenging was that my back and neck were often uncomfortably stiff.

The stiffness of my back and neck had some very unpleasant side effects. The tension in the muscles of my back and neck prevented blood flowing smoothly to my brain, which at times caused me to feel tired far more easily than I should. Given that I was travelling a lot for work and spent long days on projects, this additional physical strain often resulted in me feeling exhausted. The reduced blood flow also meant that I had to work really hard to concentrate during those times. This is a less than desirable situation to be in when you are a highly-paid consultant and expected to create solutions and plans very quickly for clients. My solution for this was to simply push myself harder and work longer hours and weekends if necessary until I found solutions no matter what. Fortunately, I did manage to do the work really well, but it was at a personal cost. I was tired a lot of the time and often felt under pressure, which made my body always feel tense. This tension affected my back and neck further.

Over a decade before my move to Germany, I made the discovery about the condition of my back, which I described in Chapter 1. After having noticed discomfort and stiffness in my back and neck for most of my life, at the age of thirty-three I discovered that this was due to my spine and neck having structural issues. I found out about the issues from an osteopath in London when he examined my back during the first appointment. However, I did not realise how severe the issues actually were until I moved to Berlin. My response to this revelation at the time set me on a path which has shaped my life from then up until today. It also, of course, led me to the writing of this book!

While living in London, I saw the osteopath regularly after the initial appointment, every two to three weeks in order to manage the effects, but I didn't know anyone comparable in Berlin. I have found, however, that if you want something and feel that it is possible, the Universe gives it to you. What do I mean by the Universe? Usually the name is used to refer to the existence of everything as a whole, including galaxies, stars, planets, humans, animals, nature, atoms, the smallest particles, space and energy. For me, the Universe means all of this and it is also a recognition that there is a power that creates and organises everything that exists. Earlier in the book when I referred to spirituality, I mentioned that some people like to call this power God and perceive it as a higher being and others refer to it as the Grand Ordered Design or energy. In this book, when I refer to the Universe, I am referring to the Grand Ordered Design.

Sometimes the tension in my neck became so strong that I actually felt dizzy – almost like I'd drank a few glasses of wine. At these times, I was unable to drive, as I would literally have been like a drunk person on the road. I also found a solution for this. Since I was usually away from home for work, I was able to take taxis or get lifts from colleagues in order to get around. Back at home in Berlin, we lived near public transport, so there was no need for me to drive. Yes, it's incredible how creative you can be when it's required of you! Obviously, all of these symptoms were extremely worrying and continued to bother me until the Universe lent me a hand!

My Spine Tries to Do a Disappearing Act

Some months after I had been living in Berlin, a friend of Eiko's came to visit and I got into a conversation with her during which she mentioned that she'd had trouble with her back in the past. Through her private health insurance, she'd found someone who had fixed her back in "no time at all". My ears pricked up. Apparently, he was a renowned osteopath who had the prestigious title of 'Doctor Doctor', as he had a double diploma. She spoke with great enthusiasm about him. That was the guy for me! Or so I thought.

I duly made an appointment to see the osteopath, who I will refer to as Herr Doctor Doctor. When I got to his office building, I found that there were two practices there. One was for the clients without private health insurance who were being funded by the public health system. It was often full of people seated on uncomfortable seats, all waiting for a long time and paying very little or nothing. The other was a private practice, which contained comfortable sofas; here, you were not kept waiting too long and paid a premium price for each visit. Herr Doctor Doctor had the private practice! During the first appointment, I was ushered into his lovely office. As I sat in the leather chair with a hot tea in hand, I explained that the reason for the visit was that I had been experiencing stiffness with my back and neck for years and that I needed treatment to alleviate it.

He was pretty tall, as many Germans are, and peered down at me through his glasses from a great height. He examined my back and neck and pronounced that first he needed X-rays of my spine so that he could get a better idea of what was going on. I was happy to go along with this. Anything to get my back sorted out!

This was the first time in my life I'd had X-rays taken of my spine, so I was totally unprepared for what was to come. Herr Doctor Doctor told me that my spine was curved to one side instead of being straight, which I already knew about. I had twisting in my lower spine, which I also knew about. It appeared that a vertebra in my neck was protruding when it shouldn't, which I knew about, too. So far, so good. Nothing new. He asked me, "Have you had an accident?" I replied, "No, not that I can remember." I could feel my old friend Fear coming up. He then told me that I had 'kinks' in several places in my spine instead of it being straight as you look at it from the front or back. I had known about this but had not known how bad it was until I saw the X-rays. Fear tightened my chest a little more and breathing became more difficult. Lastly, the X-ray showed that the bone of the vertebrae in my upper spine had started wearing away, disappearing, which I had been completely unaware of. By now, fear had a hold of me. I found it hard to breathe and started to feel dizzy.

Apparently, to have this condition where the vertebrae are deteriorating in someone of my age was not normal. It was something that happened to women in their fifties and onwards, and I was only thirty-five. Oh no!!! This revelation frightened me. My heart sank and my blood pressure level dropped to somewhere around my ankles, leaving me feeling extremely weak. So, what was I supposed to do? Herr Doctor Doctor peered at me over his glasses and said, "Well, you will have to see therapists for the rest of your life to manage the condition, otherwise it is likely to get worse". I searched desperately for a glimmer of hope as I asked, "So, it is possible that I can recover or at least stabilise the condition with treatment then?"

Herr Doctor Doctor replied, "There are no guarantees; your spine may still degenerate further as you get older. You can't grow the bone back or get it to reappear. You can only stop it wearing away further. Over time, it is likely that parts of your spine will fuse together. When they do and with this is combined the kinks in your spine, your back will become much less flexible." Well, thank you for the positive reassurance! To him, he was just being matter of fact, but to me it felt like my world had just collapsed in on me. Have you ever been given news that turned your world upside down? How did you deal with it? To me, it was as if I had been dealt a massive blow to my body. My heart sank even further, my blood pressure dropped another notch and my chest became even more constricted. I started to feel slightly nauseated.

The underlying fear I often had of things going wrong reared its ugly head at that moment. My overactive imagination started to create unpleasant images. I had pictures in my head of myself as a sixty-year-old woman, bent over in half because my spine could not support me any longer, writhing in agony from back pain, being unable to think because of a lack of blood supply to my brain, or being constantly dizzy and unable to function normally. My creative mind (fuelled by fear) had gone completely overboard in the worst possible way. In that moment, I did not know how to stop it from churning away.

But then suddenly, something else happened inside me. A feeling of hope arose in me and lifted my heart. The renowned Herr Doctor Doctor just gazed down on me from his great height of wisdom (I am 150cm tall, so most people tower over me) and emphasised that the best course of action was to stretch regularly and get regular treatment. Silly me, what did I know as a lowly consultant? How depressing! My heart sank again. But yet again, my Inner Power System (which I introduce shortly) would not accept that I was destined to rely on treatment for the rest of my life. This lifted my spirits again. Have you ever experienced a time when you felt like you were knocked flat by some unexpected piece of news? But then something stirred within you that gave you hope and helped you to cope and move ahead with your life?

Your Inner Power System (IPS)

Each and every one of us has an innate wisdom, an inner knowing and source of strength which is always there and serves us throughout our life, especially in moments when we need it the most. I call it the *Inner Power System*. Your Inner Power System is something like your own internal GPS telling you which direction to go, which turns to take and the best route to use to get to your destination pleasurably or in the fastest amount of time. It has a sense of purpose and has the ability to cut through any doubts that your brain might throw at you. It simply 'knows'. But often, the Inner Power System and its voice of wisdom cannot be heard as your brain takes over and drowns it out with doubts and the voices of other people. In that moment when Herr Doctor Doctor delivered his prognosis, my Inner Power System stirred and made itself heard. It said, 'But medicine is developing in leaps and bounds all the time. Surely in the future a "cure" will be found for my condition'. Initially, I felt calmer at these thoughts. But the fearful part of me responded back with, "I hope so, but I can't see how." My emotions were in turmoil for a brief time as this internal battle went on. However, as I described earlier at the beginning of this chapter, our reaction to unexpected events or revelations determines our future destiny.

In the end, my Inner Power System won the fight. Determined not to let this latest prognosis get me down, I vowed to find a way to heal my spine even though I did not know how that could happen. Deep inside, I just felt that there must be a way that I had not discovered yet. Have you ever had a time when no matter what you were being told by someone, you just somehow knew there had to be another solution? Years later, I now look back and I am deeply grateful for this Inner Power System, as without it I would not be where I am now and would not be writing this book! My imagination does not even wish to contemplate what my life would have been like if I had taken on board the 'expert' advice I had been given instead of listening to my innermost powerful self.

In the months that followed, I had further appointments with Herr Doctor Doctor, which helped my back and neck feel better, but only for a few days at a time. Then the same amount of stiffness as before returned. He rarely asked me anything beyond, "How are you feeling today, then?" and listened to the answer without responding. He then mechanically performed the same techniques, like a set routine, which made me feel like part of a factory production line and not like a human being, worthy of care and attention. After a while, I started to realise that his method was not really helping my back feel better beyond a few days, and I also found his manner irritatingly condescending. So, I decided to try other therapists.

Unfortunately, other therapists were even less effective than Herr Doctor Doctor had been. They all shared his view of my condition being incurable, adding to the picture of a horrible future previously created by my mind. But my Inner Power System tried to make its voice heard and refused to let me buy into what I was being told. Sadly, at that time, I did not believe in myself strongly or have my own back, and so I would often start to doubt that it was possible and start to get despondent. This internal battle carried on for a while. Just as I started to wonder whether I should give up this crazy notion of healing my back and go back to Herr Doctor Doctor and subject myself to treatments for the rest of my life after all, I received a sign that I was on the right path. Thank you, Universe!

The Eccentric Therapist

I came across a fantastic therapist in a totally unexpected way. One day, Eiko went to see his doctor about something. During his visit, he'd heard about an osteopath named Oliver who was also qualified in physiotherapy and acupuncture, combining both Western and Eastern medicine into his work. Oliver was pretty eccentric, but brilliant in his own way.

To get to his office, you had to enter through an inner courtyard. This is typical in Berlin, where the buildings are grouped together in a square and surround an open space in the middle. As I entered the courtyard, I could hear my feet on the cobbled floor. The crisp air was on my face. I felt excited, but was a little wary after my previous experience with Herr Doctor Doctor. I rang the bell and a friendly petite blonde lady let me in. As I entered the practice, I noticed that there was a narrow corridor with various rooms going off it. I sat on a comfortable seat and waited. Oliver was running late. After a while, I started to feel a bit impatient. Then suddenly, someone in a hurry appeared in the corridor from one of the rooms. He looked like a mad professor with unkempt brown hair, wild eyes and an air of being distracted. It was Oliver! 'Oh dear!' I thought. 'I think I've made a mistake.' Luckily, I was wrong.

Oliver was flying around between clients as if he did not know what he was doing. But as I discovered, this was just an illusion. He knew precisely what was going on with each person. Oliver had the right to use the title Doctor Doctor, but interestingly enough, chose not to use it. Having this title enabled practitioners to open up a private practice and make a lot of money charging higher fees. Oliver wanted to make himself as accessible as possible to everyone who needed his help and therefore had a normal physiotherapy practice. His treatments were highly effective and as a result, his practice was always incredibly busy.

Unlike all the other therapists I had seen up until this point, he asked a lot of questions before treatment in order to find out what had been happening in my life recently and in the past so that he could determine the best combination of methods to use. This was the first time any practitioner had bothered asking me these sorts of questions and it made me feel that he cared about my well-being. He asked what had been happening in my life before each session because he told me that what was happening in my life would also be reflected in my body. This was the first time I had heard this. However, as my German at that time was fairly limited, I did not get to find out much more about this.

Oliver's unique combination of therapies was the most effective I had experienced up until that time. My back and neck felt ten times better, becoming more relaxed and flexible. While all this had been happening, I had still been working as a software consultant and coping with the symptoms in one way or another. Thanks to the treatment from Oliver, I was able to work more effectively, my concentration improved so I could be more creative and I enjoyed more energy in general. It was like having a new lease on life!

The most wonderful part about working with Oliver was that from his study of both Western and Eastern medicine, he had found that the body is able to heal itself. He believed that my spine and back could heal over time. You can probably imagine my excitement at this. At last! Here was the first therapist who backed up the voice of my Inner Power System, the voice that had been telling me for a long time that it must be possible. How do you feel when a 'hunch' you have about something turns out to be right? These hunches, which are sometimes referred to as a "gut feeling", come from your Inner Power System. I felt the most tremendous sense of relief and joy.

Stirring It Up Exercise

Our Inner Power System often kicks in when we need it most. To help you become aware of how often your Inner Power System comes into play, I have created some questions below.

1. How many times in your life have you been in a situation that seemed difficult and then suddenly you had a strong feeling about what you could do to resolve it or a 'crazy' idea popped into your head?

   Then when you followed it, this feeling or idea turned out to be right?

   Or perhaps you ignored it and then wished you hadn't, saying to yourself, "I knew I should have done xyz"?

2. How many times have you been in conversation with someone who is having an issue and you somehow just knew what the issue was really about and the solution to resolve it?

   Did you share this with the other person or did you doubt yourself? Did you ask yourself, 'How can I possibly know this?' What was the outcome?

3. Have you been in a situation where you were not sure how to proceed and then somehow you just got a strong feeling about the best thing to do?

   Did you follow the feeling or did you doubt yourself? What was the outcome?

You will most probably find that each time you have followed your Inner Power System, it has provided you with the best outcome. Today, I encourage my coaching clients to follow their Inner Power System as I have learnt over the years that it will always assist you in navigating your journey through life.

Principle: Listen to Your Inner Power System

We are all born with an Inner Power System. However, as I mentioned in the previous section, we often ignore it. Why? We are often taught to do so from a very early age in an insidious way. As we are growing up, we are taught to doubt ourselves in various ways. We are taught to listen to other people – our parents, teachers, family members, people who are older than us – because they know better than we do. This is useful when we are very young and do not know much about the world and how it works. But as we grow older, we understand more about the world and do not need to rely on others as much. However, we still have this 'program' in place that effectively says 'You don't know much; you had better get someone else's opinion or you will mess up.' So when our Inner Power System speaks to us, instead of listening to it, the quiet but strong inner voice that says 'trust yourself', we doubt ourselves and make our decisions based on what we have been taught about the world and what other people are saying to us.

This is how I was for most of my life, hardly daring to trust myself. However, something still drove me to listen to my quiet inner voice and to this day, I am eternally grateful that I did. Without it, I would be leading a very different life today. One that is full of physical discomfort, fear about the future and a feeling of being unfulfilled.

Unleashing Exercise: Contacting Your Inner Power System

I based this exercise on the Quick Coherence Technique from the Institute of HeartMath and a meditation from Marci Shimhoff. When you do this exercise your body produces oxytocin, which is the bonding chemical, or love chemical, as it is also known. It will help you to bond with yourself for a few moments, allowing you to contact your Inner Power System more readily.

I suggest you read through the whole exercise briefly before doing it. Do the exercise with your eyes closed, but if you need to open your eyes briefly to remind yourself of the instructions, that's fine.

1. Place your hand over your heart.
2. Breathe normally and just observe the sensations you get by placing your hand over your heart. Notice the warmth around your heart. Let your breath deepen naturally.
3. Close your eyes and imagine you are breathing through your heart. Allow the warmth to spread from your heart area throughout your body.

4. Once the warmth has spread all over your body, ask any questions that arise for you. Some examples of questions are: "What is the key message for me?" "What do I need to know right now?" "What should I do about xyz?"

5. Listen to the answers that arise. The answers may be images or words or sentences. Keep asking and 'listening' as long as you wish.

6. When you are ready, relax your hand and slowly open your eyes. What did you learn? What messages or images did you receive?

Whenever you receive news that seems to turn your world upside down, you always have a choice as to how you react. You can let it get you down and resign yourself to 'fate', or you can take your destiny into your own hands and decide to either accept things as they are and be at peace with it or do something to bring about a change. Your Inner Power System is always available to help you make the right decision for moving forward; you just need to learn how to tune into it on a more regular basis. The Contacting Your Inner Power System method is a useful tool for doing this. Tuning into your Inner Power System is an important step in backing yourself in life and following your dreams.

Who Has Got *Your* Back?

Chapter 3: Backing my Dreams

"It's choice - not chance - that determines your destiny."

Jean Nidtech

We often have dreams that seem impossible, or perhaps we know they are possible, but we can't see or don't know how to make them happen. So we put them aside and almost forget about them. Actively trying to follow our dreams seems nonsensical, impractical, silly and even downright crazy. I have had a number of dreams throughout my life that seemed to be crazy. I already shared one of them, my dream of living in Australia, with you in the last chapter. What sort of 'crazy' dreams do you have? What have you done about them?

In this chapter, I share two of my other dreams with you. The first was to do something I really loved, which was to help people feel good about themselves and their lives. However, it seemed impractical and crazy. For goodness' sake, I was getting on a bit! I was already in my thirties, had an established career and a great lifestyle. Throwing that all away and starting a new career was not 'logical' and was highly risky at the ripe old age of thirty-something, wasn't it? Would I really be able to support myself financially and maintain the sort of lifestyle that I had gotten used to? Luxury holidays, a fabulous wardrobe, going out every weekend to the hottest places and still being able to save money and make investments.

The other dream was to get married someday. This had been a dream of mine ever since I had started reading fairy tale stories as a little girl with a vision of a handsome prince whisking me away to happily ever after! (If you are a man reading this, I wonder of you if you imagined yourself as being that prince. Most likely you did not!) As I grew older, I found that in Europe, people lived together successfully for decades and even had children without a marriage certificate. So I began to question whether marriage was necessary. At this point, I started to seriously doubt the validity of my dreams. Can you relate to this?

Something is Brewing in the Background

Around the same time that I discovered what was happening with my spine and back, I also started to notice more and more that although I still enjoyed the consultancy work, there was something else I felt that I would love to be doing. But what? I had realised while living in Europe that the part of the work I really enjoyed the most was talking to people about their personal issues.

I specialised in supply chain planning, which involved forecasting future sales, planning the effective distribution of the products around the supply network and planning the amount that needs to be produced and purchased to support the sales. It was very interesting work. Effective planning saved clients millions of Euros each year and enabled them to increase their sales.

However, on this type of project, people had all sorts of anxieties popping up. You will not be surprised to know that one of the most common anxieties people had was losing their job. As planning involves forecasting future sales, production and purchasing figures, people were afraid of being held accountable for not delivering according to the forecast figures. If the figures were inaccurate, the business could lose millions of dollars' worth of sales and also end up with excess quantities of stock they could not sell because they had produced the wrong products. They were afraid that they would at a minimum, get into trouble, and at the worst, lose their job.

People on the projects were also afraid that their job might become redundant. As planning was a more efficient way of doing things, some roles did indeed become redundant, but at the same time new roles were created. However, for the people involved it understandably created uncertainty about their future. The other common anxiety was about whether they were smart enough to embrace the new technology being introduced. If they were not able to embrace the technology, what would happen to them then? Furthermore, because the project added to their existing workload, some people got anxious because they felt overloaded. Lastly, quite often those people who may have had issues at home found that these issues were exacerbated by the extra work and longer hours. Have you experienced any of these issues? What did you do about it?

Many of the people I worked with would end up telling me about their issues and then apologise for 'dumping' on me. But I loved it. I don't mean I loved that they had issues. I loved the fact that they felt they could confide in me. I found myself helping them find solutions to make their life easier or reassuring them about their work. Over time, this aspect of my work became far more thrilling than the project work. My heart sang when the person I was with went from being anxious to feeling relaxed, when they went from feeling weighed down to feeling lighter and uplifted.

I realised that by helping them pay attention to their Inner Power System and what was happening, they could avoid feeling unnecessary pain further down the track. The same applied to me. I found that as time went on, the whole aspect of listening to people, understanding what was happening for them and helping them find a way forward was what I loved the most. But how could I make money from that? There I was in a well-paid job with lots of benefits, but my heart was not in it as much as before.

Slowly, I realised that after all these years, maybe I was not in the right role for me. I was no longer loving it. I also realised that I was not being paid as well as some of my other colleagues who had managed to negotiate better salaries for themselves. When I first got the job, my old friend Self-Doubt had got in the way of me negotiating a better salary with my manager. This made me feel terrible. Then my other old friend Fear raised its ugly head and told me that I was OLD for goodness' sake – in my thirties! You can't change careers when you are THAT old. I mean, time is ticking on. Jumping ship and trying to swim to shore would be disastrous, wouldn't it? Have you faced a similar situation in your life? What did you do about it?

So, I persisted with the consulting work. But the feeling inside me kept growing, gnawing away at me and causing me to feel uncomfortable. I kept on ignoring it. I kept telling myself to focus on doing the job really well and it would go away. So, I did the job really well, driven by a desire not to let myself or other people down, and got great feedback, which brought me some satisfaction for a while. But the uncomfortable feeling would not go away. I started to feel anxious because of the internal conflict. This happens when you are not being true to yourself and when you are doing things that you do not really want to do. Have you faced the same at some point in your life?

I told the feeling, "Go away and leave me alone! I am not about to throw my life into turmoil and sacrifice my successful, well-paying career for some ridiculous idea of helping people feel better. Helping people resolve issues in their lives. Who I am to do that and who the hell would pay me for it? It's a ridiculous idea!" But the desire still persisted and would not go away. So, this internal battle fought itself out for a while until one day in early 2003 when something totally unexpected happened.

Stirring It Up Exercise: Are You Doing What You Love?

This exercise is designed to help you reflect on where you are right now with your current occupation, whether you are employed or running your own business. The questions themselves are deceptively straightforward. However, they are questions we rarely ask ourselves because we are so caught up in 'doing stuff'.

Take a piece paper or a notebook and pen to write out the answers.

1. Are you doing work that you love right now?
2. If not, what else would you love to do?
3. What is holding you back from doing this?
4. How do you feel about that?
5. What impact is it having on your life?
6. What are you prepared to do about this?

When you reflect on your answers, you will get a glimpse of what is really going on inside you that you may not have paid attention to before, much as I did for a long time. Once you pay attention, this will lead you towards making a decision. Here, there are only two possible decisions: to take action or to not take action. I did not know to ask myself these questions previously. I did not examine what was holding me back or what I was prepared to do about it. I ended up being stuck in fear and not taking any action for a long time until I went on a trip from Berlin back to London.

Chapter 3: Backing my Dreams

"You Mean People Actually Pay You To Do That?"

In March 2003, I went to visit my brother Blaise in London to spend some time with him. Having faced the challenges of living with our parents when we were younger, the bond between us remained strong in adulthood. Blaise has had my back though much of my adult life. He has long been one of my biggest fans, always encouraging me in my endeavours. I have done the same for him. Having someone in my life who backed me so strongly helped me to pull through tough times much more easily. He believed in me even when I did not believe in myself, which often helped me to find the strength to move forward in my life. So, I decided to share my internal turmoil with him.

Blaise also worked in the software industry on major projects. He listened to me explaining that I would love to help people find solutions to the issues they were facing in their lives and to help them feel good about themselves. He then pointed out that I had actually been doing that for many years already, both at work and in my private life. Oh wow! He was right. I had! He suddenly had an idea and said to me, "You know, Chris, I've worked with this guy called Stephen who is really talented and is looking to do something in a new company. It sounds like what you've been talking about. I think it's called Life Coaching." At that point, I had never heard of it before. Blaise continued, "I don't know much about it, but it sounds a lot like what you've been talking about. I think it's pretty new as well."

My heart leapt and started pounding with excitement. So, maybe helping people as a career wasn't such an improbable idea after all! "How can I meet him?" I asked eagerly, hardly able to believe it. My brother gave me Stephen's mobile number and I called it straight away. As I waited for Stephen to answer, my heart was racing and I could hardly breathe. When he answered my call, I was so breathless and overexcited that I started babbling. My thoughts were, "Oh dear! He must think I'm a total idiot." Have you ever had one of those moments? Still, somehow he managed to understand me in spite of my garbled sentences and agreed to meet with me the next day.

You will not be surprised to know that I could hardly sleep that night. Suddenly, it appeared that maybe the thing I wanted to do was not so crazy after all. "Oh please! Oh please! Let it be what I have been searching for," I pleaded during one of the longest nights of my life. By the next day, when I met Stephen, I had managed to calm myself down. I wanted to make sure I came across as being professional and reasonably intelligent. He explained that he had been offered a role in a new organisation that wanted to specialise in Life Coaching. They were in the start-up phase. He explained what Life Coaching was and as he talked, I could hardly believe my ears. It was exactly what I wanted to do and more! I felt like I was going to burst.

"How could I get myself a role within this company?" I asked as calmly as I could. What I really wanted to do was get on my knees and beg that they take me on board. Stephen replied, "Well, you would need to get a qualification as a Life Coach first and then simply apply to work for the company." He pointed me in the direction of an organisation that offered coach training. Damn! I would have to study; I could not just get training from his company. Still, how marvellous! Unbelievable! After all this time I could start moving in the direction I wished to go. There were organisations that actually trained people in the stuff! It was like all my Christmases had come at once.

I could not stop thinking about it. I decided to take action straightaway, so I contacted the coaching school. There was a slight issue – I now lived in Berlin and the courses were run in the UK. I considered moving back to London for a while, but felt reluctant. Then it occurred to me that there may be coaching courses that were conducted remotely, so I did some research. Oh joy! I managed to find another school that offered remote learning done via the Internet and phone. Yippee! I signed up for the course immediately. When the course material arrived via post a few weeks later, I ripped open the box as I could hardly wait to get started. However, shortly after I received the course material an unexpected turn of events in following my dreams caused me to choose to delay gaining a certification in coaching for several years. I never actually started the long distance course after all and ended up returning all the material to the school a few weeks later after an exciting development took place.

A Dream Arrives At The Speed of Light

After a holiday in Australia in 1996, I fell in love with the country and had decided that I would love to spend a few years there as a beach bum, just travelling around and having fun with the surfers. Ahem! However, upon meeting Eiko, I realised that this particular vision was not going to be so easy to achieve with another person in tow. Well, at least not the surfer part. Ahem! So I revised it to one where I found a job and we could both move out there together.

In July 2003, I applied for an independent visa so we could migrate to Australia with the intention of living there for a couple of years. Apparently, this could take anywhere from a year to eighteen months to get. In Australia, the visas work on a point system. Your age, occupation, years of experience, etc. all earn you points and you need a minimum amount of points before you are eligible to even apply for a visa. To my dismay, I discovered that in order to get the independent visa, I still had to work in a field in which I was expert to ensure that I had the required amount of points to qualify for a visa.

I had to weigh up which dream was more important to me: getting certified as a coach or moving to Australia. My Inner Power System kicked in at this point and said, 'How about both? Move to Australia, enjoy the time there, work to build up some money, get certified as a coach and then after four years or so move back to Europe and do coaching full-time'. I loved this new idea! So instead of changing careers I decided to continue as a consultant and updated my skills to the latest version of the software I was working with.

I was extremely pleased at having backed myself in this way. So here I was, on track to making my dream come true. However, I was a little disappointed that it would take up to eighteen months to get to Australia. The only way to speed up this process seemed to be getting sponsored by a company. I felt that getting to Australia was totally possible and decided not to worry about how it would come about. This is when I discovered that when what you think and how you feel are in alignment, the Universe gives you what you want much, much quicker.

A month after starting the visa application process in July 2003, I started contacting companies in Australia. I found a company that needed my existing skills and was willing to sponsor me to come to Australia. They wanted me to take up a role in Melbourne as a senior consultant for a period of four years, maybe longer. I could hardly believe it – I had found a company to back me in moving to the other side of the world! This meant that instead of waiting up to eighteen months, I could emigrate with Eiko within a couple of months. As we had already prepared our paperwork for an independent visa, we had everything ready, so in this case from start to finish the sponsored visa process took just four short weeks. The plan was to move there by end September

2003, way sooner than we could have hoped. I was totally surprised by the speed at which it all occurred. However, I knew deep down that it was meant to be. The plan was for me to go first and settle in and for Eiko to join me before Christmas. Hooray! Then I received another surprise.

An Irresistible Proposal

On being granted the sponsored visa for Australia, Eiko arranged dinner at one of the most romantic restaurants in Berlin. He told me that he'd heard about it and had been wanting to go there before we left for Australia. When we got to the restaurant, we were struck by the beautiful surroundings and the wonderful ambience. Upon being shown to our table, I noticed that there were two dozen red roses in a vase sitting right in the middle. No other table had these on it, so I was puzzled as to how we had so many flowers on ours. I was informed by the waiter that they were a present from Eiko. I was even more puzzled. He did buy me flowers on occasion, but two dozen red roses was a pretty extravagant amount for him. He was obviously trying to soften me up for some reason. My Inner Power System did try to tell me that he may be about to ask an important question, but I ignored it. After all, he had said that he wasn't keen on the idea of marriage; he didn't feel it was necessary.

Eiko started looking a bit nervous. I asked if everything was all right. My old friend Fear raised its head and I started to wonder what the bad news was. He reassured me that everything was fine. So, I let myself relax and we proceeded to have a lovely dinner. Towards the end of the meal, he started looking extra nervous. 'Oh dear,' I thought. 'What's going on?' You've probably guessed what happened next, but I had no idea up until that time that he had experienced a change of heart.

You will not be surprised to read that Eiko proposed to me over dessert. He brought out a beautiful ring made of white gold with a tiny diamond in it. Simple, but elegant – just the sort of thing I love. Of course I said "Yes" and was also relieved to at last know why he had been on edge all evening! I could hardly believe it was happening. Two of my biggest desires being fulfilled at the same time – moving to Australia and getting married. I felt a deep sense of gratitude and happiness. However, life is full of opposites and there were some things which I had not considered in the middle of my excitement at having my desires come true.

Chapter 3: Backing my Dreams

The Dream Has a Slight Crack

Sometimes we are so focused on what we want that we forget that there is always going to be an opposite aspect to it. Every benefit has a drawback and vice versa. These opposites bring a balance to life, which I write about later in the book. Even though I was excited about the move to Australia, I suddenly realised something. What about all the people I would be leaving behind as I ventured forward into this bright new life? There was also a feeling of helplessness when I realised that I had my network of friends in Europe who backed me in my life. Who was going to back me in Australia? A few days later, I started to have a small sense of sadness and panic mixed in with the joy I was experiencing. Have you ever experienced this mix of emotions? There was, however, no way that I was going to give up my dream of living in Australia.

The visa and wedding preparations occurred simultaneously. A heady mix of excitement, fun, stress, frustration and sadness all at the same time. It was a crazy but amazing period of my life! We had a small wedding, with only our closest friends and family attending. The wedding itself was in the late morning, so we organised a brunch at one of our favourite cafes, followed by a boat ride on the Spree River. Then, in the evening, we had a fabulous Thai wedding dinner, followed by clubbing until the early hours of the morning. We were doing all the sorts of things we loved to do most in Berlin for perhaps the last time. The wedding weekend was absolutely beautiful, but as you can imagine was also tinged with sadness. After experiencing so much love over the weekend, I had a deep sense of loss in leaving all these wonderful people behind. Have you been through an experience where you had such mixed emotions?

Not knowing how often we would see each of them in the coming years was heart-wrenching. It was especially difficult to know that I would be so far away from my brother Blaise. My heart was heavy. This is when I realised that although it is thrilling to follow your dreams and make them come true, there can also be a less thrilling side, which you may not have considered. The day after the wedding, a lot of tears were shed by everyone. Tears of happiness for our having gotten married and tears of sadness at our moving away to Australia. Looking back now, I am very grateful for having had that time at our wedding, as Australia is very far away. Thanks to modern transportation, you can get there within a day and a half from Europe, but weekend trips to just 'pop over' and see friends and relatives are not possible! In spite of the sadness, my desire to follow my dream was strong within me, so off I flew to Melbourne a week later.

Help! I Forgot To Be Careful What I Wished For

There is a saying, "Be careful what you wish for, you might just get it". Well, I wished to move to Australia and I put my wish out to the Universe, but I did not provide any further details of what I wanted.

Normally it is a habit for me to do research before I travel somewhere. Somehow with having been to Australia previously in summer weather, the excitement of being sponsored, the added excitement of Eiko proposing marriage and the unbelievable excitement of getting married, it somehow slipped my mind to research Melbourne. In fact, when I had the dream of moving to Australia, I had never actually specified *where* in this huge land I wished to live.

As well as the structural issues in my spine, I found that when I was living in London and Berlin, the cold weather made my muscles tense and stiff, which then also affected my back and neck. I was hoping that the warmer climate of Australia would help with this. I had visions of temperatures of 24 degrees through winter and over 30 degrees in summer. This was not based on any evidence whatsoever of what the climate is like all year round in the different parts of a huge country. When I had last been in Australia in 1996, it had been in December, which is summer, and it was very hot everywhere I went. I was in for a rude awakening.

When I left Berlin, it was late September, which is autumn in Europe and spring in Melbourne. So I packed only my summer clothes, expecting to be in a heatwave. I had visions of me running around in a bikini in my free time. I did not pack anything warmer than light cardigans. (Please don't laugh!) When I landed in Melbourne, reality hit me. It was warmer than London some of the time, sure. Far warmer than Berlin in winter, definitely. But it did not take long to find out that Melbourne is not the tropical paradise I had envisaged. In fact, the moment I landed in Melbourne, it started raining and did not stop for almost a week. I thought I had gotten on the wrong plane and somehow ended up back in London. Oh dear!

In the European-type climate of Melbourne, I found that the issues with my back and neck were no better than they were back in Europe. Still, at least I was finally achieving my dream of living in Australia for a few years. Now all I had to do was find the right osteopath or, even better, a way to heal my spine. Oh, and a warm jacket to wear until my winter clothes arrived!

Getting Back on Track With My Dreams

After being in Melbourne for just three weeks, I was asked to travel to Wellington, New Zealand to work on a project for six months. How marvellous! I had always wanted to see New Zealand and now I was getting the chance. My colleagues joked with me that I would come back pregnant. I did not get the joke, so I asked them what being in Wellington had to do with my becoming pregnant. They replied, "Everything closes down at 5.30 p.m., there are more sheep than people, and there is nothing else to do out there." Wink, wink. All right, we will see what happens. As it turned out, what they said about Wellington was not true. It is a lovely place to live and is very vibrant. However, six months later, I did indeed find myself pregnant just before I returned to Australia, which my colleagues found hilarious.

We decided to call the baby Jade after the form of very dark green jade found in New Zealand. After Jade's birth, I took six months' maternity leave. Becoming a mother made me feel very differently about life. My desire to coach people grew even stronger than it was previously. The original plan to do consulting for another three years seemed like an eternity. So, I decided to embark on becoming a certified coach.

I had agreed with the company I worked for that I would go back to work part-time, working two to three days a week so that I could have more time with Jade as she was growing. On the days that I was working, I noticed that the yearning to do coaching was partly fulfilled by the fact that I was able to coach people unofficially on the projects and help them feel better about themselves, their work and life in general. However slowly, it became clear that it was not enough. I started to feel torn inside. On one hand, I had a great job and worked with some great people. On the other hand, by now I knew that rather than working on software-focused projects, I wanted to work on people-focused projects!

On the days I was at home with Jade, I was on a mission! I played with her during the day and did my studies when she had her naps, in the evenings and on the weekends when Eiko was also home. At times this did take its toll and I was pretty tired, but I was determined to not delay doing what I loved any longer. I knew that many people called themselves coaches without having a qualification, but I did not wish to be one of them. I wanted to know how to structure coaching sessions and to also learn the most effective techniques in coaching people so that I could help my clients get the best results in the shortest space of time. Yes, my consulting background did influence me! It took me eighteen months to get the qualification.

You can imagine my excitement when I received my certificate in the post. At last, I could finally embark on an official coaching career! I had my own coach around this period who was doing coaching full-time. I was very envious of her for being in this position. She backed me in the idea of me moving into coaching and gave me some practical ideas of how I could do this. Some friends also supported me in this. They saw the impact that doing work I no longer loved had on my back and my sense of well-being and were totally excited at the idea of me moving into something I did love doing. Both my friends and my coach felt that I had a natural ability to do coaching. It was great having people whom I respected backing me. But…

The problem was that I was the one who did not back myself in this. The thing that got in the way of doing the coaching full-time immediately was the fact that I earned a six-figure income working full-time and even working part-time it was a substantial sum. What would happen if I were to stop that? Eiko's salary was not enough to cover all of our expenses. My old friends Fear and Self-Doubt suddenly had a grip on me, creating less than enticing pictures in my mind. I had images churning in my head of my back getting worse and worse from stress, not being able to pay the bills, not being able to go on holidays, having to use up all our savings and being flat broke. My mind screamed at me, 'I can't do it! It's too scary!' But yet again, my Internal Power System stepped in amidst the panic and said, 'You CAN do it. Just do it part-time to start with and see how you go.' I was tremendously relieved at this new idea and decided to carry on working three days a week, doing consulting and coaching in the evenings or the weekends.

At that stage, I had a handful of clients, which meant that I could still spend four whole days in the week with Jade until she went to sleep at night. I loved it! Interestingly enough, I also started to enjoy the consulting again for a while, but it didn't last. The consulting work was not the issue, it was more that having started the coaching and getting so much fulfilment from it; I wanted more of it. Just a few evening sessions each week were not enough. I started to consider how I could do more coaching hours. There were two ways I could think of. One was to spend less time with Jade, which was a choice I was totally against.

The second choice was to cut down on the consulting hours. This was the more obvious choice, but my old friend Fear had me in its grip. I decided to do nothing. Fear temporarily backed down. However, I had no inner peace because I was not following my dream. I could sense a tension within myself, which I chose to ignore. My back and neck became unbearably stiff from the inner tension, but I still took no action except to get more frequent appointments with my osteopath. I had taken a definite step backward in terms of the health of my back.

Principle: If You Don't Pay Attention, You Pay With Pain

This is one of my favourite principles, which took me a lot practice to apply in my life! Do you realise that we often get signals from the Universe about the right action, path or direction to take in our lives? However, we often do not pay attention to the signals. Why? As human beings, our greatest fear is that of change. Take a moment to check in with yourself. How comfortable do you feel with change? If you look at children, they often feel uncomfortable with new things. Their parents usually have to encourage them to try something new and reassure them when they are facing new situations or unfamiliar places or unfamiliar people. Even as adults, we do not wish to change what we know for something we do not know. We believe that it is safer for us to stay doing what we are doing and not change anything. Therefore, we deliberately ignore the signs we are receiving that something in our life needs to be different. What often happens then is that we start to experience some sort of pain in our lives as the Universe tries to alert us to this fact!

The pain may be physical, such as a bad back, heart problems, stomach problems, skin conditions, feeling exhausted or something else. The pain may be that the life situation we are in becomes worse, such as our work becomes more difficult, we are criticised suddenly by different people or various relationships become difficult. Does any of this resonate with you? Even then, sometimes we do not pay attention until the pain is so bad that we are forced to make a change in order to survive or at least get back to some sort of 'normality'. Aaaaagggghhh! This is what happened to me. I did not pay attention until the pain became awful. What sort of pain signals have you received in your life that forced you to make a change?

For me, the mental and emotional anguish started while I was still working as a software consultant. I didn't want to pay attention to my Inner Power System that kept telling me very clearly what I really wanted to do in life, which was coaching. I kept trying to ignore it. My old friend Fear had its ugly grip on me, along with its closest friend, Self-Doubt. I had always been the main earner. How was I going to support my family if I didn't do this highly-paid work? How on earth could I make as much money with coaching as I did with consulting? My mind created all sorts of horror scenarios. We would struggle. We would starve. We would have nowhere to live. We would... No, no it's too scary!

Yes. My mind was being super creative but in a totally disempowering way. I definitely did not have my back at this time and was completely ignoring my Inner Power System. This is when I started to discover the truth of the principle that if you do not pay attention, you pay with pain. The anguish I felt inside refused to go away. I started to experience pain in the form of a body that was often tense and a back and neck that were even more stiff than they were previously. This made me feel very tired and often dizzy to the point where I felt nauseous. It made doing the consulting work particularly challenging, but I pushed myself through with enormous effort to get the work done.

There were two key motivators at this point that kept me going, the salary and the desire to not let other people down. Emotionally, I felt very heavy and as if I had some huge hole inside me which could not be filled. I received expressions of gratitude and appreciation from my colleagues regarding my efforts, but it was an *effort* for me. Where I had once enjoyed the work, now I found it to be a burden. I had problems sleeping at night, fighting with myself about carrying on with the consulting work or making a switch to doing coaching full-time. The lack of sleep added to my tiredness. But fear had its grip on me. Fear of leaving behind what I was familiar with and moving to something new which I was unfamiliar with - running my own coaching business on a full-time basis. Looking back now, it is just as well that I did not know how challenging running your own business can be at the beginning, otherwise I would never have made the transition.

My ego also came into play. In the area of consulting I worked in I was regarded as an expert, whereas in coaching, nobody knew me from a bar of soap. There were a lot of people in coaching who had way more experience than me. My ego was not too thrilled with this idea. It did not want to have to prove myself all over again after all the years I had invested in my line of work.

Due to all the travel and internal turmoil, I now needed osteopathic treatments every two to three weeks. I felt like I had taken a step backward in terms of my back's healing. But I still refused to pay attention. To make matters worse I started travelling every week at this point from Melbourne for a project in Sydney. The client and the team were easy to work with, but it was simply not enough to fill the void inside me. I reached a point where I felt like I was being torn apart and was going to have a nervous breakdown. Sometimes we have to get to a very low point in our lives in order to rise up again stronger than before. Around this time for me, the Universe lent me a helping hand in two ways.

Firstly, I caught a virus. Considering that it was autumn at the time, this was nothing out of the ordinary. Normally, I was used to being ill for a week or so and then recovering. This virus lasted one whole month and during that time I was still travelling every week between Melbourne and Sydney for the project. I felt exhausted the entire time and the stiffness in my back and neck often made me feel nauseous. Of course, I realised what the issue was. My internal turmoil of many, many months doing work I clearly no longer loved had begun to affect my cells, and my body was now severely depleted. My whole system could no longer cope, so was unable to recover from a common virus. I am used to being energetic, so to be ill for so long and feel so exhausted was an extremely unpleasant experience.

I finally got the message and began to pay attention. I realised that it was time to create a new reality for myself. Having made this decision, I began to recover from the virus rapidly and started to make plans for my future in coaching. I was still fearful of resigning from the job, but after feeling torn apart for so long and then being ill for a month, I just had to pay attention and face the fact that I could no longer carry on doing what I was doing. It was not a 'safe' option for me any longer. It was clear to me that carrying on doing something I did not love anymore would simply result in more pain.

The second way the Universe lent a hand was that I learned that colleagues who were junior to me were being paid more than me. Moreover, I discovered that in the previous three years I had been paid less than the role was worth because I had not negotiated my salary yet again! This gave me a much-needed slap in the face. Earlier in the book, I wrote that life is full of opposites. Sometimes we think we have been dealt a blow which later turns out to be one of the best things that could have happened. In my case, discovering that I had not been so well-paid as I had previously thought was key in helping me decide to let go of the work that I had been doing for over a decade. I decided that it was well and truly time to follow my heart at long last. In the face of this decision, my old friend Fear stood no chance! My Inner Power System took the reins!

Stirring It Up Exercise: What Are You Tolerating?

You can do this exercise using a paper and pen to write out the answers.

1. What are you tolerating or putting up with in your life right now?
2. What is causing you to do this?
3. What are you gaining from doing this? It may not be obvious at first but there is usually a hidden benefit.
4. What is it costing you?
5. What are you prepared to change? Pick a tiny step.
6. What would your life look like if you did make a change?

Quite often we go through life tolerating things we do not like or want in our lives because we believe we 'have to' or because it is 'easier'. Whenever we do this, we give up a part of our personal power and start to feel 'stuck' in our life which can cause us pain. By becoming aware of the impact on your life of tolerating things you do not like or want, you are in a better position to make the necessary change and free up your personal power as I did.

Current Pain Turns Into Future Gain

There are moments in our life where the decisions we make and the subsequent actions we take have a major impact on us for the rest of our lives. As I described earlier, my defining moment came when I decided to abandon the 'security' of working in an industry which I was familiar with and in which I had built up a good deal of expertise, to take a huge leap into the very unfamiliar territory of the coaching industry where I had some expertise and experience, but not in terms of running my own business.

I was fortunate to have colleagues who were intelligent, capable, caring and fun to work with. When I resigned from the job, my colleagues were shocked. "But how are you going to earn the same sort of money doing something new?" asked one, reminding me of my own fears. Another stated, "I would love to do something I enjoy more, but can't see how I could earn enough money doing it." Oh great! That's the last thing I needed to hear. I started to see the hidden fears that people have of doing something new and still being able to support their families. Many of my colleagues were definitely not backing me up in my brave new adventure. Since I had the same fears and was working hard to keep them under control, the last thing I needed was a reminder of them. I thought about carrying socks around with me so I could stuff them into people's mouths to stop them from talking!

Fortunately, some of my colleagues had a different reaction. They found it was amazing and admirable that someone with my level of experience and at my age of forty-one suddenly wanted to switch careers. This made me feel more supported. After the initial shock, the vast majority of my colleagues were very excited for me and extremely encouraging. The general comments were, "You will be great at that type of work," and "You are a natural!" Gulp! 'I hope so!' I thought to myself, 'Because I am taking the most enormous leap of faith in my entire life'.

At the time, I did not know that the day I resigned from the company where I worked was truly the first day of the rest of my life. In the following weeks, I noticed that the tension in my body that had often been present due to being under constant pressure started to reduce. This, of course, meant that my back and neck started to feel less stiff, which was a bonus. Even more wonderful was the realisation that when I woke up each morning, I was really looking forward to my day. I had not experienced this since early on in my consulting career.

Once upon a time, I had really enjoyed the work I did and loved getting up in the morning to go to work. However, it was a long-forgotten feeling. It is interesting to note here the phenomenon of how easily we get used to things. I had the feeling of, 'I guess I had better get up and get to work' for so long that over time, I had forgotten that it had ever been different. It just became 'normal' to feel this way. Worse still, other people around me felt the same way about their work too. 'Back to the grind' was a phrase I often heard. I only noticed that I used to have the feeling once it was gone! Have you experienced this at some time in your own life, where you only noticed how bad you had been feeling once the feeling changed? When I started to look forward to my day, the feeling was a total contrast. Now, years later, I am so grateful that I backed myself in spite of my fear and took this step. Every day, I wake up and I get to do what I love AND make money from it! When you do things you do not love, it affects your overall sense of well-being and, after a time, also affects your health.

Reaping the Benefits of Tuning In

The following story illustrates what happens to your body when you do something you do not love and instead have negative self-talk occurring, and then what happens when you make changes to turn this off and tune in to yourself. One of my clients came to me for coaching because he wished to reduce the amount of stress he was experiencing. He was also often ill, had low levels of energy and felt pretty flat most of the time. He did not realise at first that he was doing work that he did not love and was also tolerating many things that he did not enjoy. He was so busy trying to get things done that he never stopped to tune in to himself and ask himself why he felt so flat at work. He put up with doing many tasks that he did not want to do and when he did not get everything done he beat himself up with negative self-talk for not performing well.

When I asked him how things were going at his workplace, he was overwhelmed. He told me about all the things he did not get done and how much stress this was causing. He also told me how unhappy he was with his performance.

From personal experience, I know what it does to the body when you talk to yourself negatively and force yourself to do things you do not enjoy most of the time. This causes the body to start to shut down. I realised that he was not backing himself in life and that he had rarely done so in the past. Given this background, it was appropriate to take small steps to change this so as not to further overwhelm him. So, we came up with a plan for him to make some small changes that would bring immediate benefits and help him to start to back himself more.

The first step was to get him to appreciate himself. I asked him, "Do you realize the impact it has on your body when you speak to yourself in a negative way?" He replied that he did not and asked what happens. I told him, "It affects the cells in your body. It causes your body to shut down, which means you lose energy and feel tired all the time even if you are not ill. Additionally, if it carries on over a long period of time, it also affects your immune system, which leads you to becoming ill more frequently."

He had not made the connection between his thoughts and how his body reacts before this. He recognised that what I described had been happening to him. He was taken aback and asked what he could do instead. I suggested, "You could start communicating with yourself in a more positive manner and you will find your energy returning and will fall ill less frequently."

He asked me for some ideas of how to do that. The first thing I suggested was that he make a list of all the things he had managed to get done in the last few months at work and at home. He wrote the list and was astounded at how much he had achieved. When I asked him to check in with his body and see how it was feeling, he told me, "That's amazing! I feel so much lighter already!" So we agreed that his next key action would be to acknowledge the things he got done at the end of each week and to congratulate himself to ensure that he maintained a sense of self-appreciation. As a result of this, he stopped speaking with himself negatively after first realising what it did to his body and he started realising how much he actually did get done on a regular basis.

The second thing we did was to sort out how he used his time at work. He very rarely took breaks, as he felt 'I have so much to do' and was alarmed when I suggested taking frequent breaks during the day. I explained that taking frequent breaks of only ten minutes every hour or so would actually help him re-charge his battery and also help him to focus better, so he would actually get more done. He found that he could cope with just ten minutes, so he started taking regular short breaks to make better use of his time. After he started taking these small breaks, he was astonished to find that his energy levels and concentration were indeed better.

A third change he made was to not say "Yes" to everything he was asked to do, but to consider whether it was actually part of his role. Doing this reduced the amount of tasks he did not like and cut down some of his workload as well. With these small but fundamental changes, he noticed after a while that his stress levels had reduced dramatically and he had a lot more energy. This meant that he could think more clearly and this is when he realised that he did not actually like the type of work he was doing! He decided to back himself and asked his manager for a transfer to a different department, doing more of the type of work he enjoyed the most.

At the time of my writing this book, my client has not been ill in the last twelve months, his energy levels are better than ever and he is enjoying his work far more. After continually backing himself in the past year, he has gained additional confidence and started to tune in to his desires more. He discovered that there are other things he is passionate about which he had never considered that he could make an income from. Tuning in and focusing on the area he is most passionate about, he is now considering starting his own business within one of these areas. What a wonderful turnaround!

Unleashing Exercise: Tuning in To Your Inner Desires

Like my client, many people are so busy 'doing things' that they do not get a chance to tune in to what they really desire. This exercise has three parts to it, which lead into each other in order to help you tune in to your desires. Before you start, note how your body feels – how tense or relaxed it is. Take a piece of paper or a notebook and a pen. Write out the answers to all the following points.

1. Write down and complete the following sentence:

    If I did not have to worry about money, I would…

    Keep writing until you run out of things to write. Be completely honest with yourself, as no one is looking over your shoulder.

2. Write down and complete the following sentence:

    If I had absolutely no fear, I would…

    Keep writing until you run out of things to write. There are no right or wrong answers. There are simply YOUR answers, so tune in to yourself.

3. Review what you have written so far. Are you already doing any of those things now?
4. If not, what is getting in the way of doing any of them?
5. What are you prepared to do about it?
6. What is the first small step you can take?
7. When will you take this action?

Now that you have tuned in to yourself, notice how your body feels now. Tuning in to your desires and deciding to take action no matter how small the action is gives you a quiet sense of power.

Many times in our lives, we do not follow what we really desire, letting fear hold us back. When we do this we are not fully living a life we love. When we choose to do this, we are not backing ourselves and we do not have a sense of our own personal power. Unfortunately, we then also do not get to experience the joy and sense of fulfilment that comes from being connected with our own personal power. Instead we remain doing what we are doing and that becomes our reality, causing us to feel 'stuck' in our lives. 'Life is OK', 'I feel a bit flat, but that's how it is I guess,' 'I feel like there must be something more to life,' are comments that I have often heard. When we choose to back ourselves and free our personal power, we can create a brand new reality for ourselves!

Who Has Got *Your* Back?

Chapter 4: Backing a New Reality

"We are all here for some special reason. Stop being a prisoner of your past. Become the architect of your future".

Robin Sharma

We have the power to create whatever we want in our lives, but we often don't realise it. We are taught from an early age that the world works a certain way and that we have to fit into it, otherwise we will be on our own or will face great difficulty. So, we resign ourselves to tolerating things that do not enrich our lives, unaware that doing so hides some of our personal power from us. This then becomes part of our reality. However, resigning ourselves in this way makes life far from pleasant. After a while, we are so used to living like this that we do not realise things could be different, so we make no attempt to change what is happening in our lives. We develop a type of amnesia, where we forget what it feels like to have the flow of life pulsing through our bodies. When I was younger, I lived in a reality that said the world was a harsh place to live in and that I was worthless.

Principle: Reality Is What You Make It

What is reality? OK. I know whole books have been written on this topic! What does it mean to you? In my opinion, reality is whatever we perceive it to be. We live in a world that we think is real. Why do I say this? Well, if you think about it - how we view the world is based on what we learned about the world as children, and it forms our reality. However, each of us has a different view of the world based on our upbringing and our experiences while growing up. How do you view the world? However *you* view it is your reality. So, which view of the world is 'real'? Yours or mine? The answer is that what is 'real' for each of us is only based on our perceptions. So what I perceive is real for me and what you perceive is real for you. I have read various references to reality therefore being considered as being an 'illusion'! What do you think?

In simple terms, if we received support and love while growing up, our reality is likely to be that the world is a friendly, caring place and that we are capable of anything and cannot fail. Having this view makes life much easier, of course. If we felt unsupported and unloved while growing up, our reality is likely to be that the world is a dangerous, uncaring place and that we are not good enough and we had better be careful or we will fail. Having this view is going to make life somewhat harder. Of course, what I have written is about the extremes. For the majority of people, the way they view the world is a mixture of these extremes of support and challenge, depending on what they experienced while growing up.

Our reality then impacts the way we experience life. If, for example, we perceive that we are capable of anything and cannot fail, when we don't like something in our life, we will either take steps to change it or change the way we perceive it so that we can accept it. On the other hand, if we perceive that we had better be careful or else we will fail, we will struggle to make changes and feel like life is difficult and not feel so great about it.

Earlier in the book, I mentioned that once I moved to Melbourne, one of my first tasks was to find myself an osteopath. But the people in my office did not know one, so when one of them recommended her chiropractor, I duly went to see him. I was asked the same questions as usual, which by now were part of the process for me. 'Have you had an accident?' etc. When I asked him whether he could help me to heal my back, he was non-committal and emphasised that I would need regular treatments with him, probably every few weeks. I immediately felt uncomfortable with him. When I asked who would pay for these, he got flustered and said, "If you have private insurance, most of this is covered, otherwise you have to pay the full amount yourself." I told him that it was a lot of money for me to pay out and not knowing how many treatments I may need made me feel uneasy. I realised how fortunate

I had been before in Germany as these treatments had been fully covered by my health insurance, but as I was feeling pretty dizzy and tired from the stiffness in my back and neck, I booked some appointments with him.

Unfortunately, my back and neck did not feel much better after these treatments. When I commented on this to him, he gave me a vague response which did not reassure me at all and then tried to book me in for more sessions. I realised that I had two choices: to feel sorry for myself or to take action. My Inner Power System kicked in and helped me to make a decision. So I decided that I did not wish to waste any more time or money with him. I then tried various other practitioners who were more helpful, but did not have the level of skill that my osteopath Oliver in Berlin had. None of them believed that my back could be healed and I found the treatments were often mechanically performed. I had the feeling that although they cared about my well-being to a certain degree, their biggest concern was to get me in for as many appointments as possible, as it was good for their business. I felt a bit despondent.

At this point, my reality could have turned into something like, "I doubt that I can find the right practitioner in Melbourne to help me. Maybe I should go back to Oliver in Berlin." However, my Inner Power System spoke, telling me "Don't give up. You will find a way to help yourself." I decided that instead of feeling helpless and at the mercy of other people, I would create a new reality for myself. I would ask the Universe to help me find a fabulous practitioner who believed as I did that my back could heal and would help me to do it. This decision to ask for help paid off!

My Quest for Healing Receives a Boost

I kept trusting that the right practitioner would turn up. Sure enough, in the next few months I came across a gifted osteopath, Aleksandra Hristov. Aleks combined osteopathy with her own unique art of healing. The thing that struck me the most about Aleks was the vibe of warmth, that she exudes. When you meet her, you are instantly enveloped by her warmth and when you walk into her practice room, it is as if you are being cocooned by it. It makes you feel safe. I had never experienced this with any therapist before, not even Oliver in Berlin.

I told her that I wished to heal my spine and neck and she replied that she believed it was totally possible to do that. In the ten years since I had discovered the issues with my spine, she was only the second person backing me up in the quest to heal myself. Unlike many of the other therapists I had seen, she sought to help me to help myself as much as possible. Where had she been all these years? I wondered. But I knew the answer. I had never actually asked for someone like her before!

I was thrilled! At last I had come across someone in Melbourne who was willing to work with me to help me heal myself. Someone who was not trying to keep me dependent on her services. Unlike other therapists I had seen, I had the feeling that she genuinely cared about my well-being. She did not try to get me in for another appointment straight away, whether it was actually required or not. Much of the time, she would advise me to come in when I felt it was necessary. She told me, "You know yourself really well, so I will leave it down to you as to when you want to come in." As a result, I really felt like she had my back and I developed a friendship with her, which remains to this day.

Have you had someone try to keep you dependent on them? When this happens, it means that they have a degree of power over you. You feel that you cannot do without their help or else you will be in trouble. There are some professionals who attempt to create this sort of relationship with their clients so that the clients then keep coming back for more and more appointments. What they and their clients do not realise is that in doing so, the personal power of the client becomes hidden. When you are dependent on someone else, you cannot access your personal power. You start to believe that you are not able to help yourself without the assistance of the other person. This then affects your ability to trust yourself and lowers your self-esteem.

In relation to therapists, when you learn ways to help yourself you do not need so many appointments or have to pay so much money. You start to tune in to yourself and trust yourself. Being able to trust yourself and not depend on someone else creates a sense of empowerment. It gives you a strong feeling that you have your own back, which is extremely beneficial for your life.

Chapter 4: Backing a New Reality

Joining the Dots of My Spine

I learned a lot from Aleks about the body's ability to heal itself. The first thing Aleks would do before starting any treatment with me was to ask a lot of questions about what had been happening in my life. I learnt that when you become stressed, overly busy or emotionally upset, it results in the tightening of the muscles in various parts of your body. This occurs for everyone. Apparently when certain muscles in your legs and arms become stiff, because of the interconnection of the muscles in the body it causes the back and neck to also become stiff as well. Later in the book I describe something called the 'fascia', which is an important part of the interconnectedness of your body.

You will not be surprised to learn that whenever I felt stressed or became very emotional, the worst tightness appeared in my upper back and neck. Up until that point, I had known that there was such a strong connection between what the mind thinks, the emotions that get triggered and then how your body reacts. Understanding this connection helped me to become aware of some of the core emotional issues that were triggering the stiffness in my body overall.

Aleks showed me stretches I could do to alleviate the stiffness in key parts of my body. She also showed me breathing techniques that I could use to relax my body overall and release pent-up emotions. Whenever your emotions become 'stuck' in your body, your energy does not flow around properly, causing you to feel unbalanced and 'not quite right'. By breathing into parts of your body, you can release emotions that are stuck there and ensure that the energy flows around more easily, which in turn helps keep your muscles in a more relaxed state.

As Aleks treated me, I became aware of physical sensations in my body. At times it was as if I had mini-whirlpools in my body. At other times, it was as if the sea was inside my body, the water flowing towards the shore and ebbing away. When I commented on these sensations to Aleks, she smiled and explained that it was the energy in my body moving around and releasing built-up tensions and emotions. She explained that your past experiences from your life are stored in your body, especially if they were upsetting in some way. During the treatment, some of what is held in your body gets released and you become more relaxed and at peace. Wow! I had known all of this. I found it very exciting.

The curious thing is that the physical sensations I experienced came up almost every time I had a treatment with Aleks. It occurred to me that this had never happened with any of the other therapists I had seen previously. There was obviously something she was doing that caused this to happen. When I asked her about this, she explained that when she works with her clients, she seeks to connect with them at a deeper level, the mind, body and spirit level. Then Aleks made a revelation that totally blew me away. She said, "Christie, the reason why you find what I do so powerful is because you are doing it with me. If you were not so open to helping yourself, you would not get such strong sensations of movements occurring in your body as you release old stuck emotions and energy. It's you who is doing a lot of this work; I am just facilitating."

My mind found it incredible and struggled to comprehend it, but my Inner Power System said to me, 'This just feels so right. Somehow, I knew this already.' I felt my chest expanding out and my heart opening up. A huge wave of warmth washed through my entire body and a profound sense of peace came over me. I was in awe of what I had discovered and also very grateful. So I was also doing the work to heal myself, not just Aleks! How wonderful! I felt the tears running down my cheeks as a deep sense of gratitude engulfed me. At long last, I was on the path to healing my back. Following this appointment and conversation with Aleks, I started to tune in to my body more when I was meditating in the mornings and I found that some of the stiffness which had built up in my back would dissipate, leaving me feeling more flexible. This resulted in my needing fewer appointments. Hooray!

Supporting My Self-Healing!

This was when I first experienced the ability of the body to heal itself. You can imagine how excited I was about this discovery. However, at this point I was still expecting that I would be working with Aleks and additionally helping myself through meditation and breathing exercises in between visits. As I described above, I learned to breathe into certain parts of my body. To my amazement, I discovered that when I focused on a particular part of my body and breathed into it, the area would immediately become more relaxed. You can try this for yourself. If you feel tension in any part of your body, focus on that part and 'breathe' into it. You will notice the tension softening and it may perhaps disappear altogether. When there is less tension in your body, your energy flows around much better. This means that you feel more energetic and can think much more clearly. This clarity helps you to make better decisions and create more of what you want in your life.

In my case, I started to feel more peaceful within myself as I released a lot of tension and at the same time the stiffness in my back and neck became a little less severe. As the flow of energy in my body improved, I was able to focus better on my daily tasks. I found that I was also able to see what was happening in the lives of the people around me more clearly. This put me in a better position to help them to find solutions for some of the issues they were facing much quicker. This aspect of my work started becoming increasingly important for me.

You Can Heal Your Life!

Around the time I was starting to understand the connection between the mind and body, I came across the wonderful book *You Can Heal Your Life* by Louise Hay that I mentioned in Chapter 1. Up until that point, I had a vague awareness of the connection, but after meeting Aleks and also reading the book, I suddenly became fully conscious of it. The issues that I had with my spine and back came from not feeling loved and supported in my life when I was younger and continued as I was growing up. As I read the pages with fascination, I started to reflect on whether I now supported myself in life and realised that in many ways, I did not. I realised that throughout my entire life I had often not backed myself and not listened to my Inner Power System. I had let fear drive many of my actions or more accurately – reactions.

As I read the book it became clear to me that the way I had not been supporting myself in life was literally affecting my back, thus causing all the symptoms I had experienced up until that point in my life. But knowing this was one thing. The question I had was - what could I do to help myself further? I was doing the breathing exercises and I was also working with Aleks to release negative emotions and trapped energy to improve the health of my back. However, I only saw her once a month so the going was slow.

I knew deep down that I wanted to do more work to help myself release my 'negative' emotions and beliefs. My Internal Power System gave me the feeling that what I wanted was entirely possible. Earlier in the book I stated that when your thoughts and feelings match, you get what you truly desire in life. Not long after I had put out the desire to help myself more, I met Benjamin J. Harvey, who showed how I could do exactly that. I write more about this later in this chapter.

Stirring It Up Exercise: The Power of Your Mind-Body Connection!

This is an exercise used in Neuro Linguistic Programming (NLP) that demonstrates how rapidly the thoughts in your mind affect your body and how you can also use your body to influence your mind.

1. Think of something that makes you feel sad or that you do not particularly like. Notice how your body is feeling. Notice your posture.
2. Now think of something that makes you feel really good or that you really like. Notice how this makes your body feel. Notice your posture.

That is how strong the mind-body connection is. Your thoughts have an immediate impact on your body!

3. Now look up at the ceiling and smile. Keeping your eyes looking up at the ceiling and while smiling, try and think of something sad. Try as much as you want. You will find that it is not possible.

This exercise is a small example of how strong the mind–body connection is. And that it works in both directions. Whenever I do this exercise with some of my clients, they are always surprised to find how quickly they feel uplifted just by changing their thoughts or looking at the ceiling and smiling. It helps them to be more aware of the sort of thoughts they are having, knowing that there will be a physical consequence for them, too.

A New Life Mission Emerges

By 2008, I had completely fallen in love with the idea of helping people feel good about themselves and their lives. I fantasised about how wonderful it would be to wake up every morning and know that you are going to make a difference in the world. That you are going to help people feel better mentally, emotionally and physically. The desire to do this became stronger over the next two years and I wanted to help all the people in the whole world to overcome their pain, reduce their levels of stress and discover how wonderful they are. In those early days, I was on a mission to save the world!

Since then, I have revised my mission in life drastically! The world does not need saving. Even if it did, there are plenty of people out there trying to do so in one way or another. Now, my mission is to inspire people, to help those who wish to be helped in creating a life that they love. In doing so, there will be a group of people in the world who are living life on purpose and loving it! I see these people in turn positively impacting the lives of others around them. This way, there is a multiplication effect of the number of people in the world who are living a life they love.

This multiplying effect is demonstrated by one of my clients who worked in a drug withdrawal unit where people are often in crisis. I first met her when I ran a weekend course covering the foundational aspects of NLP. After learning about the fundamentals, she understood better how people develop as they grow up and it gave her an insight as to how some of her clients had ended up in their current situation. She also learned some techniques to help people change their way of thinking about themselves and the world.

This client went back to her workplace and started to put into place some of what she had learned from me on the course. She combined what she already knew with what she had learned. Initially, her manager was not too thrilled with her attempting to introduce something new to the centre when there was no evidence that it would work. However, my client decided to back herself and went ahead and did the work anyway. It had the most profound impact on her clients. They went from feeling like they were stuck in a hopeless situation, to viewing themselves and the world in a much more positive light. As a result, they started to turn their lives around and started on the long road to recovery.

My client told me that their taking more charge of their lives made them feel much stronger and better about themselves. This led to less worry and pressure for their families. Not being consumed with worry about the person anymore meant that their family members were then able to move on with their own lives and feel better. That is the story as far as I know it. You can imagine the impact that each of the family members would have had on the lives of the other people they knew, leading to potentially 70,000 people being impacted. All this stemmed from one person who backed herself in introducing something new into her workplace! Since then, she continues to back herself even more by developing work which will, as she puts it, "bring light into dark corners"! How many more thousands are going to be impacted directly and indirectly, I wonder? It's wonderful!

When you consider the hundreds of people that you know, you will see that a positive change in you has a ripple effect that extends beyond just your immediate family circle to these hundreds of people, and even further than that. The first step in making such a difference in the world is having your own back!

An Exciting Encounter With Another Man

While I was still working with Aleks, I had another encounter that further deepened my belief that I could heal myself and also showed me a way to do it. In 2008, I met a talented coach and mentor, Benjamin J. Harvey, whom I mentioned earlier. We connected with each other, but it was not clear to either of us how or even if we were meant to work together. Around that time, I also discovered that I was able to do energy healing with people, but did not know what to do with it. Interestingly enough, around that time, Ben was known as the Energy Guy!

Having never considered myself as a healer, it was exciting for me to find that I had this ability. It was also fairly unnerving, as I did not know much about this whole area. So I avoided doing any hands-on healing with clients and just used it to help friends. Somehow, I felt unable to back myself in doing the healing on others, as I thought I did not have enough knowledge. Have you experienced a situation where you did not help people because you doubted your ability or knowledge?

Then I bumped into Ben again in 2009. By that time, I knew what I wanted to do - grow my coaching, healing and training business and expand my knowledge regarding working with energy even further. How very interesting, then, that the Energy Guy pops up in my life just as I decide to look for a new coach and mentor! I was so excited! Out of all the coaches I knew and the ones I had previously worked with, Ben was the only one who had walked down the path I also wished to go down. He had established a very successful coaching, healing and training business. That's the guy for me! So I decided to invest in myself and my business and engaged his services as a coach and mentor for the next three years. Ben's knowledge of healing and human transformation was astounding and I took full advantage of what he had to offer. Apart from his knowledge, he had a wicked sense of humour and the sessions with him were a lot of fun. I was like a sponge, soaking it all in. He also had a successful sales background, so was able to give me many great ideas on how to expand my business. I definitely made sure that I got my money's worth from him!

The 3 Step Self-Mastery Program is Born

Since establishing my coaching business, Crystal Clear Horizons, in 2006, I had coached a number of people on personal, work, life and business issues. Sometimes people booked single sessions with me to resolve a minor issue and other times anything between six to twelve sessions on focusing on a particular area of their life. I loved the fact that I could help people resolve their issues really quickly. It gave me a real buzz that they were then able to start backing themselves more in life. However, I felt that there was more that I could help these people with. What I really longed to do was to help people find their purpose, discover their full potential and to start creating an amazing life for themselves. This was simply not possible in one to six sessions! One day, I expressed my frustration to Ben and he gave me the idea of packaging up the coaching and healing into a full program. Fantastic idea! I had never thought of that!

I immediately decided to create a twelve-month program with clearly-defined steps. The key aim of the program was to help people to become masters of themselves. Of course I was driven by my own painful past where I had not been master of myself and as a result had not led the type of life I wanted. I saw a vision of a world full of people who were masters of themselves and were living a life they loved. How wonderful would that be? Driven by this vision, I completely rewrote my website content and coaching documents to reflect this new offering and started to market it as The 3 Step Self-Mastery Program.

It was incredible! My coaching revenue doubled within just twelve months. As you may have guessed, that in itself was totally exciting! But what was even more exciting for me was one particular session with Ben that had the most profound impact on my life. In fact, it changed my life forever! It brought me to where I am today and to the point of writing this book.

A Life-Changing Revelation Freaks Me Out

During this particular coaching session I was discussing healing with Ben, in particular the idea of healing yourself of physical ailments. I shared with him that since working with Aleks on releasing negative emotions that were trapped in my body my back had started feeling a lot better.

Ben was quiet for a moment. Then, he told me the story of a man who had one leg that was significantly shorter than the other by 6-7cm. As a result of this difference, he walked with a bent spine. Then Ben went on to tell me that this man had eventually managed to grow the bone in the shorter leg so that both legs were more even. "How did he do that?" I asked in astonishment. "Using reiki and the profound belief that he could," came the reply from Ben. My mind went into shock. What?!?!?!? How is that possible? Ben continued, "Christie you can be your own guru. You don't need anyone else. You don't need to spend all those hours and dollars going to osteopaths and other therapists. You just need to focus and form the profound belief that you can heal yourself." My head went into a spin. After all these years of searching for ways to heal my back and neck. After all this time feeling that there had to be a way that all the experts I had consulted had not yet found. Here it was. The answer was within me! I replied, "Oh my goodness, Ben; that means that all this time I have been looking for other people to help me when really I have the power to heal myself."

One moment, I was totally elated. The next moment, I was really annoyed. The bastard! How is it that he didn't tell me this before? He had been coaching me for over a year and had shared some great stuff with me but he had never said anything like this in that time. "Ben, why didn't you tell me this before?" I asked, half indignant. His reply took me by surprise, "Because you were not ready to hear it. Now you are." Of course he was right. I would have been totally freaked out by this a year earlier or even a few months earlier. I was freaked out now!

Working with Aleks had already set me on the path to healing my back, but that was with a lot of support from her. Doing the healing on my own was a totally new realm for me. One which almost overwhelmed me. How wonderful! How mind-blowing. How scary! How would you have felt in this situation? This then became my new reality – being my own guru. It was both empowering and frightening all at the same time. Why was it frightening? The answer to this lies in my background, which I will share with you later in the book in Chapter 5.

Following the conversation with Ben I found a profound belief forming deep within me that I could heal my own spine. I took immediate action. I usually meditate first thing in the morning on a daily basis, and at times I was breathing into the parts of me that felt tense. Now following my meditation I started to send healing energy down my spine on a regular basis. I could feel the energy pulsing along the length of my spine and as I did so the tension in my back would often ease even more than with meditation alone. With time the tension gradually became less. The dizziness and nausea I had experienced on a regular basis hardly occurred anymore. This meant I had far fewer problems with being able to drive. Prior to this when the tension in my back increased it caused me to start feeling nauseous and dizzy and I knew it was time to get an osteopathic appointment. My osteopathic visits became far less frequent, dropping from between two to four weeks to every four to five weeks. This was a huge feat in itself!

What was even more wonderful was that my concentration also improved greatly and in addition to coaching my clients, I was able to write and deliver more workshops. I felt like a dream was coming true! Here I was on a path I had been desiring for a number of years – healing my back, doing coaching and running workshops that helped people change their perception of themselves and their life so that they could enjoy their lives more.

I was careful with whom I shared the information about self-healing, as I knew many people would struggle with it, especially if they had never come across the idea before. So, I only told Eiko, my brother Blaise and a few other people close to me. I was happy enjoying the discovery for myself and the sense of peace that came with it. There was also something that I noticed within myself. I felt absolutely no need to 'sell' the idea to other people. For the first time in my life, I did not feel the need to seek validation or confirmation from other people. At this point I recognized that something in me had changed. I had taken a quantum leap on the path to backing myself in life!

We have been conditioned from birth to believe that other people know more than we do. Our parents, our teachers, people older than us. When we are very young, this is true. We do not have as much life experience as our parents and other adults in our lives so we grow up with the belief that we are somehow not capable of helping ourselves. We need someone else to do it for us unless the adults in our lives help us gain confidence in ourselves. Coming from this background, the thought of taking responsibility for ourselves and our bodies is scary. The reason it is scary is that humans fear their own power.

When as children we form the belief that we are somehow not capable of helping ourselves without the assistance of someone else, suddenly deciding that we have everything we need within us triggers fear. Fear can keep us safe at times, but at other times it holds us back in life. We are afraid of feeling and showing the intensity of our power. I read somewhere that "We are afraid that we will come crashing down if we fly too high or be burned by our own flame". One of my favourite quotes of all time is 'Our Greatest Fear' by Marianne Williamson. The start of the quote is the part that is most relevant for this book:

Our deepest fear is not that we are inadequate.

Our deepest fear is that we are powerful beyond measure.

It is our light not our darkness that most frightens us.

We ask ourselves, who am I to be brilliant, gorgeous,

talented and fabulous?

Actually, who are you not to be?

Many people have an in-built fear of gaining more resources, power, influence and success. We fear it because we feel that we somehow don't deserve it, or fear that at some point we are going to fail in some way. Gaining power and success means that we may have to make changes in our lives. We may have to do things differently to how we did them before. This triggers our feelings of fear. Additionally, the people in our lives may not react positively to these changes. The fear of change is considered to be the number one fear that humans have. This means that what we are really afraid of is the changes we may have to make based on discovering our own personal power.

I Get A Glimpse of Heaven

Following the conversation with Ben, I started to notice very clear evidence that when you fully commit to something and trust with your whole being that it will happen the Universe lends you a hand. You start to experience synchronicity. Synchronicity is when you experience two or more events which are related to each other in a meaningful way. They may happen at the same time or one event may follow another. Not long after the conversation with Ben, I met someone else who increased my knowledge of self-healing even further.

I do not particularly enjoy working on my own every day so I put it out to the Universe that I would love to find a group of like-minded people to work with one or two days a week. The Universe delivered! A friend of mine, Michelle Jarman, had bought up a new business called Prana House in Melbourne. Prana House is a very special place that offers yoga classes and also has therapists who work with alternative therapies.

The street Prana House is located in is not fantastically attractive, which makes what you find inside even more amazing. You go up a flight of stairs and as you do the sound of soothing music caresses your ears and the smell of scented candles fills your nostrils. When you get to the top of the stairs, your eyes focus on a space that can best be described as "heavenly" as the floors, walls and high ceiling are all white, complete with long, white billowing curtains. Around the walls are benches with richly-coloured cushions on them. People are stunned by the space. Then you are greeted by a warm, friendly member of staff. How would you feel if you got to work in such a beautiful space every week? I was that lucky person!

Michelle asked me if I was interested in offering life coaching and meditation and also running workshops from there. I could hardly believe it! I nearly jumped out of my skin with excitement! It was like a dream come true. I started as the resident life coach and meditation teacher, which meant I was there two days a week and ran my workshops several times during the year. It was one of the most wonderful experiences for me since I started my own business to be working in such an environment.

Then one day a new practitioner called Mike Melling-Williams joined Prana House. He was a Network Chiropractor. Network is a gentle method of chiropractic that teaches your body how to correct itself. This is my interpretation of what it is. There is no 'cracking' or strong manipulation used as with other therapies. Instead, the practitioner uses gentle, specific touches on your body, to help it release long-held tensions by itself. These gentle touches bring your brain's attention to the areas of your body that are holding on to tension, and encourage your body to release it. When the body is misaligned or holds tension, then the flow of energy in your body is not as smooth and your ability to heal yourself is reduced. My understanding is that releasing the tension frees your nervous system and enables you to achieve a greater level of healing.

One day, Michelle announced that Mike was offering every practitioner free treatments so that they could get to know what he does. Of course, with my insatiable appetite to learn about healing techniques, I was one of the first people to take up such a generous offer. The first thing Mike did was to ask me to get an X-ray done so that he could see what was happening structurally with my spine. When he got the X-ray, he explained what impact each of the vertebrae has in the body if they are not in a perfect condition. I had never heard any of this before. I could relate to every single thing he told me regarding symptoms such as brain 'fog', lack of concentration, sugar cravings, dizziness and nausea. That explained why I had been feeling so dizzy and couldn't concentrate for so many years!

Knowledge being one of my highest values in life, I was soaking it up like a sponge! He also showed me exercises to release tension and reconnect with my body. I realised that when I had recently started to send healing energy down my spine while meditating, I had actually been connecting with my body already. What Mike showed me helped me to connect with my body further. After this, I started to feel even better and could feel the energy flowing much better overall in my body due to all the work I had been doing up until that point. Since, incredibly, I didn't even have to pay money for the knowledge and treatments from Mike, I decided to pay in kind. I offered him reciprocal coaching and also referred clients to him. How amazing is it that this person turned up in my life just as I was ready to become my own guru?! As stated earlier, there is no such thing as coincidence, but there is such a thing as synchronicity. This is illustrated further in the next pages.

Chapter 4: Backing a New Reality

I've Got to Move It, Move it!

My time with the Network Chiropractor was short-lived, as I followed my dreams again. I had wanted to live in Sydney for a long time. Before moving to Australia, it was the place I had wished to live in, but I had been offered a position in Melbourne. Since then there had been possibilities to move to Sydney, but something had always gotten in the way or, to be more accurate, I always LET something get in the way. First of all, I had my daughter, Jade. Well, we'd just had a baby so we couldn't move. Then my husband Eiko felt that we had only just gotten settled in Melbourne, and needed to get comfortable there. Then Eiko set up his own business and we couldn't move because he was just getting set up. Then Sydney was an unfriendly place, so why move? We got over that one when we found out it wasn't true. In any case, we realised that wherever we had lived – London, Berlin, Wellington, Melbourne – we had always managed to attract friends, so we could be confident we would be able to do the same again in Sydney, plus we already had a lot of friends there, anyway.

Then one day, it was the middle of a wet, bleary winter in Melbourne and I felt I'd had enough. I had left Europe and moved thousands of kilometres to escape this type of weather and to have more of an outdoor lifestyle. What the hell was I doing here eight years later?!?! To pacify the fans of Melbourne who may feel offended – I will state here that it is a great city with great people but it is a very personal thing and it just wasn't doing it for me.

In that moment, I made the firm decision internally that I would move with or without Eiko. This was not about breaking up with him, as I had no desire to end my relationship with such a wonderful man. But it was about what I deeply and truly wanted for myself. What I deeply and truly wanted was to live somewhere beautiful with a warm climate for most of the year and to be outdoors. I was absolutely deciding to back myself in life on this one, even if it meant the relationship with my lovely husband had to take a backseat. I was clear in myself that I was willing to have a long-distance relationship if necessary with him in Melbourne and me in Sydney with our daughter Jade. I decided to tell him within the next few days that I was moving. Then something incredible happened.

A few days later, it was cold, rainy and dark outside and we were at home. We started talking about the fact that we had been in Melbourne for eight years at this point and about how nice it would be to experience living somewhere warmer within Australia and being outdoors more of the time. Then Eiko said, "We have been here long enough. Time for a move. What do you think?" I could hardly believe my ears. Eiko saw the stunned look on my face and misread it. "Don't you like the idea?" he asked. My response was, "Darling, I am ecstatic! I so want to move!" Then I explained my decision to him. "Well, thank goodness I want to move, otherwise that would have been very difficult!" was his bewildered response. He has known me long enough to know that once I make up my mind I make it happen – and that I would have moved with or without him! In that moment, he was relieved that he had been the one to suggest the move first. As you are probably aware, when you fully commit to something and trust that it will happen you experience synchronicity. This is because your thoughts and feelings are in alignment. What sort of 'coincidences' have occurred in your life?

Manifesting My Dreams Again

So at the beginning of January 2012, we flew to Sydney to look for a place to live. Before we went we made a list of all the things that were important for us in terms of a place to live, such as three bedrooms, two bathrooms, close to a primary school, close to the water, close to the city centre, within thirty minutes from the airport and so forth. We planned to spend one week there trying to find a place to live. We were flying out on a Tuesday and returning the following Tuesday. I told Eiko that I was putting it out to the Universe that by the time we got on the flight back to Melbourne on Tuesday afternoon of the following week we would have a confirmed place to live. Our friends thought we were being over-ambitious. We didn't know Sydney and the suburbs that well, so they told us we would need time to find where we wanted to live. The period after New Year's would be very quiet in terms of rentals properties on the market because people were still on holiday. It's a competitive market because many people want to live in Sydney. Sydney was more expensive than Melbourne, so we would need more time to look and find something affordable, etc.

Chapter 4: Backing a New Reality

But there was my Inner Power System again telling me, "Don't pay any attention to anyone else. Ask and it is given. Focus on what you want no matter what and trust that it will happen. Just focus on visualising that you will have confirmation of a place to live before you get on the plane on Tuesday afternoon." So I decided to back myself and did just that.

We looked at a number of places all over Sydney before I said to Eiko, "I don't like competing with other people. Why don't we do things differently?" He was confused and asked me what I thought we could do. "Why don't we ask for private viewings where there is no competition?" He wasn't so sure. "But they have set viewing times." But my Inner Power System was out in full force and I replied, "Leave it to me." I called the estate agents and explained that we were looking for a three-bedroom property, had great references, could pay a deposit and first month's rent immediately and were leaving on Tuesday so needed to view the property before then. The key thing is that all of this was the truth, no deception was involved! We were shown several properties in private viewings where there was no competition and found an apartment that met all of our main criteria on the Monday, plus it had a swimming pool. But we still needed the confirmation so I went into a space of trusting like never before and refused to contemplate any other outcome. There was some running around on Tuesday morning to sort out the paperwork and chase up the references, but by lunchtime as we were driving to the airport, we got the confirmation that we had the apartment! Phew!

So many times, we all doubt that we can have what we wish for. When you are clear on what you want and then give yourself the feeling that you can have it, your thoughts and feelings are in alignment. This is the key to manifesting your heart's desires. But instead of being clear on what you want and focusing on letting yourself feel it is possible, you start to doubt it. You listen to the opinions of others telling you it is not possible instead of listening to your own Inner Power System. This causes a misalignment between your thoughts and feelings. So the Universe puts things on hold for you until the two match. This is the reason why so many people do not get what they wish for quickly if at all. What you wish for gets delayed and in some cases, it may not arrive at all.

Upon our return to Melbourne, we packed up everything ready to move. Our friends in Melbourne were completely thrown. Why did we want to move to Sydney? Did we know people there? What about the business? What about our daughter and school? I had a sense of history repeating itself. I realised that what for me seemed to be a logical thing to do – if something in my life is not working to change it - was pretty scary for a lot of people. A lot of people would rather stay with the safety of what they know rather than venture out into the great unknown. Earlier in the book I wrote that the number one fear humans have is that of change.

People have often told me, "You're so brave." I don't see it like that. Since I started to back myself more in life, for me the pain of living something I don't love and slowly dying a little each day is way more frightening than the temporary pain of moving towards something new that I do love or have the potential to love. I am always a little bit fearful of moving into the unknown. This is normal for everyone. As you have read, I let this fear hold me back for long periods of my life during my past. The thing that pushes me through this fear nowadays is the realisation that my time on this planet is limited and if I don't take action now to create what I truly want I will run out of time and it will be too late. My greatest fear of dying is regretting what could have been, feeling that I did not back myself and live my life to the fullest. What is your greatest fear? As it turned out, the move to Sydney proved to be one of the best decisions we ever made!

My New Year's Resolutions Become Real

What sort of resolutions do you set for yourself each year? I usually set ones with personal and business goals. At the beginning of 2013, after being in Sydney one year, for the first time in my life, I decided to set 'healing my spine' as a New Year's resolution. You may wonder why I had not done this before. It had simply never occurred to me! Time to take charge and back myself even more. I wanted to continue on the path to being my own guru. As you are probably aware, you get what you wish for. Sure enough two other significant events occurred for me a few weeks after setting the resolution for healing my spine.

In 2012, I had come across a lady named Akasha-Ka Meritamum in the U.S. who does various forms of healing. You have probably noticed by now that I have an insatiable curiosity about healing and love finding out about all the wonderful techniques that are out there. It gives me great joy to experience something new, benefit from it personally and then use it to assist my clients, friends and family. I was experiencing some sort of resistance to doing more presentations, more writing and producing videos. The usual methods I use to help myself did not change it. I could not pinpoint what the issue was so decided to try a healing session with Akasha to help me with it and also add to my knowledge bank. At this point, I ask you to keep an open mind, as what I am about to share with you may be considered as being 'Out there'.

Due to the time difference between Australia and the U.S., the healing occurred while I was asleep. Upon waking up, I noticed that I felt far more grounded than I had the previous few weeks. Akasha had also sent me an email where she described what had occurred and what she had seen during the healing she had performed on me. A key part of the email said that she saw a shadow on the lower part of my spine. "I saw a huge black spot with a thin layer of darker blue around it. It stretched from near the base of your spine up to your mid-back." It was a blockage.

Given that all the X-rays showed I mostly had issues in my upper spine, I found this confusing. So, I asked her how that was possible. Then came the first revelation. The issue with my spine was related to pain and fear. Akasha told me that the block she saw went from my root chakra up to my heart chakra and represented a toxic build up from previous experiences of pain and fear in my early life. The root chakra is near the base of the spine and is tied to our sense of tribe and the heart chakra is connected to our emotions and love. This block prevented the energy flowing through my lower chakras (energy centres) up to my higher chakras and also prevented my spinal fluid flowing properly. Both these things combined impacted the health of my upper spine and caused my upper back and neck to become very stiff.

Akasha told me, "What comes up for you is paralysed by fear which is still a result of past issues." Basically, my old fears were blocking me. Oh wow! I had experienced a lot of fear as a child and whilst growing up and there was no doubt in my mind that some of those fears were still around. Have you ever had something resonate with you so deeply that even though on a logical, mental level it sounds crazy or weird, some part of you just knows that it's true? Well, her words resonated with me so deeply that it was like a jolt of electricity going through my body. Every hair on my body stood on end (OK, I have long hair, so not the ones on my head, but my scalp *did* tingle very strongly) and I had goose bumps all over. I just knew that here at last was an insight into what had actually caused my spine and back to be in the condition that they were.

Up until this point, I had been aware that the issues with my upper back had to do with me not feeling supported and loved, but this was on a more detailed level. The mystery behind my physical condition was suddenly being unveiled. My head started spinning and I could hardly focus for the rest of the day. I had found a new focus for my self-healing efforts – healing past pain and fear that were still affecting my present life and more importantly my spine and back. So, my New Year's resolution was already underway!

Forty-eight hours later, I received the second revelation. I had agreed to swap a Life and Wellness Coaching session for a Traditional Chinese Medicine (TCM) consultation with an extremely knowledgeable practitioner, Sohial Fazam. During the consultation, I told him that I had issues with my spine and that I was working on healing it. I asked if he could recommend anything I could do in terms of TCM to help myself further.

Sohial informed me that in TCM the kidneys are affected by fear. If you experience fear and trauma as a child under the age of seven your kidneys are adversely impacted. This, in turn, means that your spine doesn't receive the nutrients it needs. The spine can deteriorate in women later on in life, especially in their fifties and when menopause starts. However, the age at which it started, or more accurately, the age at which I became aware of it, was an indication of the severity of trauma I experienced and caused my upper spine to deteriorate way earlier than it should.

Upon hearing what Sohial said, it was as if stars were exploding in my head. How incredible! I could hardly believe that I was hearing the same message again coming from a different angle. There was no denying the significance of what I was hearing. It was clear that my focus needed to shift to have a stronger emphasis on healing the emotional level. Have you ever experienced a time in your life when your whole world felt like it had been turned upside down but in a positive way? A time when what you thought you knew had to be drastically reassessed? This is what it was like for me following the conversations with Akasha and Sohial. I was excited and bewildered at the same time. How would you have felt in the same situation?

So many years spent wondering how I could have possibly developed these issues with my spine and back. So many years believing there was a way out there to heal my back myself or someone out there who could help me to heal myself. So many hours spent in despondency when I let myself lose faith and lost sight of this belief. Only daring to believe after my conversation with Ben

Harvey two years previously that I myself with the help of the Universe could heal my spine. Only knowing how to work on healing myself after Aleks, Ben and Mike had shown me the techniques.

These tremendous insights into the cause of the condition of my spine and my back sparked a new resolve in me like never before. I had already realised that to help others I had to first help myself. In the preceding seven years I had already healed a lot of fear and trauma from my childhood in my desire to become an inspirational coach and to create a life I loved to live. Now I realised that there was deeper work to be done in order to also further heal my spine and back.

I liken it to excavating, where you uncover the layers on the surface which are normally easy to access and remove and then reach the lower layers which are harder and take more effort to remove. The lower the layers the harder they are to access. I had already uncovered a lot of the surface layers, now it was time to uncover the lower layers. With this understanding a deep peace came over me. When you know that you can have anything you want by forming a strong belief that you can have it and trusting that you will have it, it gives you a tremendous sense of empowerment. In that moment of insight, I felt the strength of my personal power.

Don't Stop Me Now!

Whenever we desire something, the Universe is ready to give it to us. Ask and you shall receive. However, as I stated earlier, our thoughts and feelings must match. What we desire and our thoughts about it must be matched by the feeling that we can have it, otherwise there is misalignment. This is also referred to as "offering resistance". Instead of letting what we desire flow smoothly to us, we offer resistance by feeling it may not be possible, having doubts and thereby blocking the flow. What happens is, the Universe sees our desires, is ready to give us what we want, but whenever we are not in alignment the thing that we want is put on hold. What we desire is delayed until what we think and what we feel matches.

As you will have seen from the journey I have shared with you, although I was clear that I wished to heal my back, my feeling that it was possible did not always match. Even though at some level I knew there was a solution, at times doubt and despondency would creep in, meaning that I was not always in alignment with my desire for a healthy back. So for many years, I did not get the thing I desired as I kept finding therapists who did not help me much at all and I often did not know what to do to help myself. When we come into alignment, then 'bang' just like magic, our hearts' desires start to appear. Have you ever had this happen to you? When something you wanted for a long time suddenly shows up? This has been the case for me in the last few years.

I have also noticed another phenomenon that occurs. When you wish for something and then it doesn't show up, you sometimes forget about the thing you wished for. Strange as it may sound, this also means that your feeling about the thing you wished for is then aligned with your thoughts! When you are not thinking about it you are also not offering any resistance. So some time later what you wished for turns up out of the blue. This happened to me regarding the writing of this book. I had a strong desire to write a book two years previously but then had no idea what I could write about so forgot about it.

In October 2012, I started a reciprocal coaching and mentoring relationship with the lovely Martine Casagrande, which is on-going at the time of writing this book. One week it is my turn to be coach and mentor, the next week it is her turn. During one session in March 2013, I was relating to Martine the insights I had received from Akasha and Sohial regarding my back and how the condition had been caused and how astounding it all was.

Martine remarked to me, "Christie, you have acquired so much knowledge on the journey to healing your spine and back, and your life, and used what you have learned to also help so many people. You have even helped me on numerous occasions. Have you ever thought about writing a book so that you can share some of this knowledge with a wider audience?" Oh my goodness! The book I had wanted to write two years ago. I had forgotten about it! Now with the latest insights regarding the condition of my back and how to further heal it, the desire to write a book could be turned into a reality because I knew what to write about!

However, I had never written a book, the idea of what I wanted to write about was new, I didn't know anyone in publishing, I didn't know anything about the whole publishing process and so on. Some years ago, all of this would have thrown me into panic and doubt. I admit that there was a slight nervousness present. This is the sensation of doing something new in your life. However, I had a deep desire to share what I had learned with a wider audience in order to help the readers with their own life journey. This desire was so strong that it outweighed any doubt that may have arisen from my lack of experience. My Inner Power System said 'Make it happen!'

The lack of doubt was also a reflection of how tremendously far I had come on my journey in backing myself in life. As a result, I had a deep feeling that it was absolutely possible for me to write the book, get it published and become a best-selling author. My determination to make it happen was unshakeable, as you are holding the evidence in your hands right now! Have you ever had some dreams or desires that you thought were 'crazy'? What did you do about them?

It's amazing how things start to show up when you totally align yourself with an idea. After having made the decision to write the book and given myself the feeling that it was absolutely possible, I realised that I needed someone who would help me get the book going as soon as possible and keep me moving so that I could publish it in months rather than years. Through being a coach, I know that the bigger the project is, the more room there is to procrastinate and drag your feet, no matter how badly you want something. To my joy, I suddenly realised that I already knew someone who could help me! Through Facebook, I had become 'friends' with someone who was renowned for helping budding authors get their books written and had a flair with words.

I lost no time in contacting Emily Gowor, who was also known as The Word Artist, to ask her how I could engage her services. After an initial conversation, Emily agreed to take me on as a client. She offered me a structured and comprehensive mentoring package and best of all, she was available immediately. You can probably imagine my excitement! In the past, I have experienced self-doubt with any new project and then pushed through anyway, but this time I didn't need to. It just felt so right to be sharing knowledge and inspiring people in their lives. It showed me how much I have started to back myself these days!

Who Has Got *Your* Back?

Chapter 5: Back to the Past

"Life is 10% what happens to me and 90% of how I react to it."

Charles Swindoll

In this chapter, I cover the key events that contributed to my Model of the World. At this point, I find it appropriate to share with you how I came to be so fearful and so full of self-doubt that for much of my life, I did not back myself. Whenever we experience fear in our lives, it prevents us enjoying whatever is happening in our lives right now. It pulls our thoughts towards what happened in the past and what might happen in the future. When we are caught up in our thoughts about the past or the future, we cannot possibly appreciate the beauty that life has to offer right now in this very moment. When we judge ourselves or others, it also prevents us from appreciating and enjoying the present moment, poisoning it. Fear and judgement take the sweetness out of the present moment and leave bitterness behind. However, we were not born with either judgement or fear.

One of my favourite authors, Marianne Williamson, writes in her book *A Return to Love*, "We were taught to think thoughts like competition, struggle, sickness, finite resources, limitation, guilt, bad, death, scarcity, and loss...We were taught that we're separate from other people, that we have to compete to get ahead, that we're not quite good enough the way we are," and "Love is what we were born with, Fear is what we learned here." That is especially true of my childhood.

The people in my life had been taught to judge themselves and others harshly as they were growing up. They, in turn, led me to believe that I was not good enough through constant criticism and judgement because that is what they had learned. Then, after being conditioned in this way for years, I started to criticise and judge myself and others because that is what I had learned. In the culture I grew up in, it was normal to get children to behave by instilling fear in them. This was done though a system of scary stories of what happens to 'bad' children and also through threats of punishment for 'bad' behaviour. The definition of bad was never clear, so you were never sure whether you were actually being bad. Growing up in this environment, I went from being a joyful child to one who was fearful. The adults who used this method had been taught the same things themselves as children, so they were simply using what they had learned. They had no idea of the impact that teaching a child fear has on them and how it later affects them as an adult. The following section provides a brief overview on how we develop from birth. It is a simplified view rather than a technically-detailed one written with the aim of providing you with some background and insight for the following chapters.

The Stages of Our Development

When we are born, we are perfect. We know nothing about the world. In the very early part of our life, between the ages of zero to seven, we are like a sponge soaking up everything about the world around us. Colours, shapes, language, the concept of parents, family and friends. As humans, we have something called the critical faculty, which helps us to determine whether something is valid or invalid. However, before the age of seven, we usually do not have enough life experience for the critical faculty to be able to discern what we take on board and what we ignore, what we regard as being valid or invalid. This is the period when our values in life and our early beliefs about the world and ourselves are formed without too much question or challenge from us.

If we were often told "You are a naughty boy" or "You are a bad girl," we believed it because we did not know any different. If we were told that something which happened was our fault, whether it was or not, and were then punished for it, we would often not question it and instead would feel bad about ourselves. At this early stage of our lives we already started to view ourselves as being less than perfect. If we had experiences that frightened us or people in our life that frightened us we will believe that the world is a scary place. These beliefs can then persist into adulthood unless we change them along the way.

Later, between the ages of seven to fourteen, we have more life experience, which develops our critical faculty and increases our ability to discern. We start to decide what we wish to take on board and what we wish to ignore. We start to decide whom we wish to use as a role model and emulate from the people in our lives, in society and the media. If we are told something new about ourselves such as that we are "good" or "bad", right or wrong, we are much more likely to question it then than when we were under the age of seven. But at this stage, we already have the programming from our early childhood instilled within us.

The things that happen during these early stages of our life help us to create our own ideas about what the world looks like and how it works. This is also called our "Model of the World" and it affects how we experience the world. Based on this model, we start to assess and judge events, people, situations and most importantly, ourselves. However, our assessment and judgement are influenced by what we were taught by others around us as we were growing up. If we were told negative things about ourselves, we will start to judge ourselves and also others based on this.

If we experienced issues that were not resolved during this early part of our life, they will often resurface when we are adults. For example, if we were often criticised as a child, we are likely to believe that we are not worthy. Gradually, we will start criticising ourselves and then will also criticise others because that is what we have been programmed to do. When you hold the belief that you are not good enough or worthy, it affects your view of life and your perception of what your place in the world is. This can result in you feeling incomplete and uncomfortable – as if something is missing. As these issues often resurface around our forties, some people face what is called a mid-life crisis.

For me, I felt that I had nothing to offer the world for a large part of my childhood and teenage years. This made it difficult for me to form close friendships and left me feeling isolated. Once I dissolved the beliefs I had formed about not being worthy, I started to see that there was a tremendous amount that I had to offer the world. As a result, I formed and still have wonderful close relationships with a number of people in my life and great relationships with my coaching clients. Best of all, I have a wonderful relationship with myself!

I would definitely have been one of those people facing a mid-life crisis if I had not already started to work on healing myself by resolving and dissolving the negative programs I picked up when I was younger and the hurts I experienced. Thanks to this work, my forties are proving to be the most empowered period of my life so far!

Stirring It Up Exercise: Your Model of the World

We all hold beliefs and fears. Often we are so used to having them that we hardly even notice that they are there but they drive our behaviour and affect our experience of life. Take a piece of paper or a notebook and a pen to write out the answers to the questions below.

1. What beliefs do you hold about yourself? E.g., "I am not smart." "I am not creative. "People find me boring."
2. What beliefs do you have about the world or life? E.g., "There is not enough to go round so I had better grab my share." "You can't trust anyone." "You had better behave or you will be punished."
3. What fears do you have that you are aware of? E.g., "Afraid of being happy in case something bad happens." "Afraid of being alone." "Afraid of failure."
4. How do these beliefs and fears affect your behaviour and your life?
5. Where might these beliefs and fears have come from?

The above exercise is designed to make you aware of your beliefs and fears. Awareness is the first step to working to change things that are not adding to your sense of personal power.

Raising Children the Not So Good Old Fashioned Way

I was born in a small village in Goa, India on 14 October, 1966 (just in case you want to send me a birthday card or message) into a Roman Catholic family and lived there until I moved to London, UK at the age of seven. As was typical in those days, we lived with one of my grandmothers; in this case, my mother's mother. My grandfather had died a long time before at the age of thirty-six, leaving my grandmother to look after six children. In those days, the way to raise children to behave themselves so they could become a "good" person was to frighten them, threaten them and physically beat them.

In our family, telling children scary stories to force them to behave was a favourite pastime for the adults. Were you told scary stories when you were younger? How did you react to them? If the children didn't 'behave' in the way the adults wanted them to, it was perfectly acceptable to smack them on some part of the body with the hand or a stick. I was always a very bright child. This went down well when it related to getting good marks at school, but not always so well at home. I was often asking questions about the way things were done, what adults told me and how I was expected to behave. I couldn't understand why things had to be a certain way and was keen to find out. These questions were seen as a challenge by the adults around me and in those days, children were not supposed to question the 'wisdom' of their elders. Any challenge I dared to pose was rewarded with a painful whack on some part of my body. Of course the adults in my life at that point were living in their Model of the World. They were living according to what they had been taught themselves. None of them realised the disempowering effect this has on a child.

As described earlier in Stages of Our Development, between the ages of zero to seven, you are like a little sponge, soaking up everything. Your critical faculty, which helps you discern and assess what is good for you and what is not, is not fully developed so you tend to accept most of what you are told by others. The combination of scary stories and physical punishment at this age resulted in me becoming very fearful of not being loved, not being safe and of not being good enough. At that young age, my Model of the World was that it was an unfriendly place where love was in short supply and if you were not good enough, you didn't get your fair share. Do you have this feeling at times of somehow not being good enough? You may be surprised to learn that is a very common feeling. I already had a strong sense of not being good enough which started before the age of seven and persisted into my early forties.

It was accentuated when my mother gave birth to my younger brother when I was three years old. My grandmother told me (yes, I can remember back that far) that if my mother didn't bring home a brother for me from the hospital, she would throw me in the well from which we drew our water every day. I was petrified for several days until we went to the hospital, which was quite a ways from our house. On the way there, my heart stuck in my throat. I asked my grandmother, "Granny, now that I have a baby brother, you won't throw me in the well, will you?" My grandmother, who of course had not been serious about the threat, laughed and said that she would not. At last, I could relax! But the damage had already been done. From that time onward, fear built up in my subconscious in layers. The world started to become an increasingly scary place to live in.

When my mother came home from the hospital with my brother, she told everybody that the pain she had experienced at birth totally disappeared as soon as she saw that she had a boy. My mother also told me that I'd have to look after my baby brother from now on. In those days and especially where I lived, boys were more valuable than girls. Boys were the ones who would look after the parents later in life, whereas girls would get married and go to live with the husband's family. Women were also generally considered to be weaker and inferior to men. So I started to be ashamed of being a weak, inferior girl and afraid of not being loved. I wanted to be a strong, valuable and much more loved boy. This caused me deep sadness before I was seven years old. I was already judging myself as somehow not being good enough and unworthy, but not knowing what to do about it. What did you learn about being a girl or a boy when you were younger? What impact did it have on you?

In Chapter 3, I described that in early 2013, I learned that according to Chinese medicine, if you experience fear and trauma as a child under the age of seven, your kidneys are adversely impacted. This, in turn, means that your spine doesn't receive the nutrients it needs, which causes it to deteriorate way earlier than it should. In my case, this meant that in my late teens, I could already feel the impact on my spine and found in my mid-forties that the bone in my upper spine had deteriorated to an alarming degree. But on reflection now, the foundations for the issues with my spine and back had already been laid when I was a toddler.

There is Nothing to Fear But Fear Itself

In her book *A Return to Love*, Marianne Williamson writes, "Love is what we were born with. Fear is what we learned here," after we were born and as we were growing up. Fear is a natural protection mechanism that is designed to keep you safe. It is said that you only come into the world with two fears – the fear of heights and the fear of loud noises, as part of the natural mechanism for self-protection. However, when experiences in your life lead you to become fearful of life itself instead of being beneficial and protecting, fear can become detrimental and hold you back from living a full life. It prevents you from following your dreams and feeling fulfilled.

At a less obvious, dare I say, more insidious level, fear eats away at you, undermining your confidence and your ability to back yourself in life. Sucking you of vital energy that could be used instead to fuel your efforts of creating a life that you love to live. In my case, fear literally ate away at my spine causing the bone in my vertebrae to deteriorate. Many doctors I have come across are unaware of the mind-body connection. They treat the physical symptoms without addressing the underlying cause, which is often at a mental and emotional level. A close friend of mine is a qualified General Practitioner (GP). She trained in both Western and Eastern medicine and says, "Western medicine focuses on sickness. Chinese medicine focuses on wellness." Which means that people go to their doctor to stay well – a preventative approach, rather than waiting until they are ill – a reactive approach. As part of this approach to life, she recognises that fear is the cause of much illness in the body.

In the past, I used to wonder what would have happened if I had known more about the mind-body connection and the effects of fear on the mind and body many, many years ago and done something about it. Now I am very aware that much of what I have learned on the journey of healing my back would not have happened, I would not have been able to help the great number of people I have helped and also this book would not have existed if things had been different. Everything is perfect!

The Priest and His Hell

When I was growing up in Goa, you had to pay for children's education. This meant that there was a lot of pressure from parents and family members for the child to do well in school, as otherwise it was deemed to be a waste of money. As a child, I had to regularly sit for exams. Being one of the brightest in the class, I would often come first or second in each of the exams. There was a beautiful girl in my class who would be the other one to come first or second. If I came second or lower in a subject, the reaction at home was, "Why didn't you come first?" When I did come first, the only reaction was "Good." There was very rarely a "Well done!" This type of competition with my classmates and lack of positive encouragement on the home front deepened my sense of not being good enough. I also felt that I was not smart enough and that unless I came first, I was not loved. Have you had these types of feelings at some stage in your life? How did they impact you?

I was also envious of the beauty of a girl in my class. She got all the attention. Why couldn't I be as beautiful as her? So, I also formed the belief that I was not beautiful and that I did not deserve love because of it. But all the while, my little heart ached and longed to be loved exactly as I was, to be appreciated, to be admired, to be praised. Unfortunately, this did not happen.

To add to this whole scene, if our teacher was away, we were taught by the local priest. He was a well-meaning man trying to make sure that young minds were set on the right path to be free of sin. However, his way of doing this was to terrify the children into the 'right' behaviour. So, when he took the class, he would put up paintings. The paintings were beautiful with rich colours and attention to detail. Unfortunately, the content of the paintings was less than beautiful. They depicted pictures of hell, where devils were dancing around, torturing sinners who had been sent to hell for their bad behaviour.

As very young children under the age of seven, we would observe the scenes of hell with fear in our hearts, dreading that we would end up there if we did not behave ourselves. It was not always clear though what counted as being a 'sin'. Did pretending we had eaten all our dinner when we had given some to the cat or dog count as a sin? Did taking an extra sweet or lolly without asking count as a sin? Did asking adults the wrong questions count as a sin? Well, they got cross, so it must be pretty bad. It was all very confusing. I became more and more afraid of somehow doing the wrong thing. The only guidance I could turn to was to listen to what adults told me because they understood about 'sin' much better than I did. I so did not want to burn in hell for my sins like the people in the paintings.

The priest literally put the fear of God into me so much that I dreaded going to school if I knew my usual teacher was away. I used to feel nauseous and on occasion actually throw up after a lesson. One day I ran away, as I couldn't stand it anymore. My grandmother could not understand what the problem was. In her time, priests were held in the highest esteem, as they were the servants of God. So after giving me some food to replace what I had thrown up, she took me back to the school. I begged and begged her not to take me back, but she was convinced that I was being taught how to lead a sin-free life and felt it her duty to make sure I listened to the priest.

I now know that this fear that had been programmed into me contributed to the issues with my back. In Chapter 1, I described how issues with the spine are to do with the support you receive in life and issues to do with the upper back are to do with lack of love and emotional support. I certainly felt unloved and unsupported on innumerable occasions before I had turned seven. When in your life have you felt unsupported? How did it impact you?

Reflecting back on that time now, I can relate to the priest. He learned his beliefs from the environment he grew up in. His Model of the World was one where God was worshipped and the Devil was a great source of fear in people's lives, where heaven was up above and hell was down below. Nobody ever told him that we can create heaven and hell within us depending on our beliefs and the thoughts that stem from them. He was only teaching the children what he himself had been taught and believed, not knowing the detrimental impact it would have on some of them. I am certain he was convinced that he was saving young souls from eternal damnation. He did not know that showing children how to love themselves and others was far more helpful in setting them on the right path in life. You can only do your best based on what you know at any moment in time. He was doing his best. Still, I am very grateful that I ended up moving away from this unhealthy environment.

Being Ahead of the Pack

One of my dreams as a very young child before the age of seven had been to live in London, speak English fluently and wear high heeled (tick-tock) shoes. I told my grandmother that when I was older, this was what I was going to do. She would laugh and call me "crazy child" for having such unrealistic dreams. But that did not stop me from dreaming.

Earlier in the book, I mentioned that when what we desire is matched by a feeling that it is possible for us to have it, we are in alignment and the Universe delivers. At the age of seven, that particular dream came true for me. In January 1974, I found myself on a plane flying to London with my mother and brother to meet my father, who was already living there. I could hardly believe it was happening! I was actually going to London where sophisticated people who spoke fluent English in a beautiful accent lived. And I would get to wear 'tick-tock' shoes!

The wonder of it all, however, was short lived. Firstly, London at that time of the year was freezing. Having lived in Goa up until then, it was a big shock to my system to feel so cold. Then at school, I was one of the few children with darker skin and at first the other children didn't want to play with me. Worst of all was the fact that my parents were not used to looking after children. My father had been absent for most of my earlier childhood, as he had been in the British Navy and was overseas most of the time. His idea of raising children was one where "children were to be seen and not heard". So, if we said anything he did not like, he would slap us on the face or smack us on some other part of our body.

My mother was not naturally maternal and back in Goa, she had relied heavily on my grandmother to look after the children. Now she had to look after two children on her own. Looking back, I recognise that being uprooted from an environment which I was familiar with and where I felt loved by my grandmother and other family members to one which I didn't know and where I felt unloved by my parents caused any feelings of fear I had up to that point to deepen further.

Some six months after my arrival in London, I started to develop breasts. I did not understand the significance of this at the time. All I knew was that my parents seemed to find it odd and did not know what to make of it. In the meantime, my parents were both working, so they decided to make me responsible for my younger brother. If he did anything wrong, I would get punished for it as being the older child, I should know better. In my mother's eyes, he was the golden child, so anything he did wrong, it must be something he had learned from me. It did not occur to her that between the ages of seven and nine, I was also a child who had very little idea of how to look after another child.

The curiosity with my ever-growing breasts continued at a harmless level until two years later when I started menstruating at the age of nine. I was terrified at the bleeding between my legs, but I did not dare tell my mother for fear of her punishing me in some way, so I used tissues to soak up the bleeding. Then one day, we were at Easter mass and I sat on a step with my legs open. In that moment, my mother spotted that my underwear was bloody and turned her wrath on me and became very angry. My blood ran cold. I knew I was in trouble. As soon as we got home from church, she told me that I was a freak. "Look at you, you are busting out on top and dripping underneath. You are like a huge buffalo." I felt sick, but there was no compassion from her. My father doted on my mother, so he backed her up in most things. In any case, for him it was the mother's job to bring up the children, so he left it to her judgement much of the time. It was a terribly lonely, frightening part of my life where my whole existence seemed to somehow be wrong and I didn't know what to do to make it better.

I realise now that my poor mother was frightened out of her mind. In her Model of the World, girls started developing breasts and menstruating around the age of thirteen or fourteen. In her world, I was a total freak of nature. There she was in a foreign country, with people who looked down on her because of her skin colour, away from people she loved, working in a menial job, with two children to look after. Then one of the children develops totally abnormally. In her time, if your children had something wrong with them, it was a source of shame for the parents, as it reflected badly on them.

My mother was scared and ashamed of what was happening and did not know what to do. It is no wonder that she was often attacking me. By attacking me verbally and physically, she temporarily released some of the fear and shame she felt. It helped her to cope with her feelings of vulnerability. However, attacking someone else is not a permanent solution to removing fear and shame. Letting go of these feelings and replacing them with love is the only permanent solution. My mother did not have anyone in her life to help her to do this.

On reflection, I realise now that this period of my life imparted me with an understanding of what it is like to be different than the norm. What it is like to be ahead of the pack, both physically and mentally. This has made it easier for me to help my clients and friends feel more comfortable with their own difference and even better, to actually appreciate being different. It also taught me to rely on myself and this has made me very resilient in life, for which I am very grateful. I needed this resilience for the next episodes of my life.

The Kindly Uncle

When I was growing up in Goa, as a mark of respect you would refer to older people as 'Uncle' or 'Aunty', even if they were not related to you. It created a feeling of respect and community, as almost everyone is then a part of your family. When I was nine years old, an "Uncle" who lived abroad came to London to work and would sometimes stay with us overnight. This particular "Uncle" was fun and seemed to be kind. He would bring us presents and be nice to us where our parents would often be criticising us.

One day after dinner I was sitting in the kitchen drinking water and everyone else was in the living room. It was boring being around grown-ups, so I was happy sitting by myself for a while. The 'Uncle' came in to fill up his whisky glass. Then instead of going back to the living room to join my parents, he stopped and looked at me with a strange look in his eyes. He saw that I was alone and said, "Good girl. Nice girl." I was surprised. My parents very rarely told me that I was good or nice, instead, they were so critical of me that I was often in tears. The 'Uncle' came closer to me and started to touch my breasts. It hurt and I asked him to stop. He simply repeated, "Good girl. Nice girl." I so wanted to be a good girl and here was my chance to prove I could be. But why did it have to be so painful? Maybe it was better to remain a bad girl and not have the pain. Then he said, "Don't tell your mum." Of course I wasn't going to tell her and get blamed for something yet again. Looking back, I now realise that he saw how my parents treated me and knew that if he was 'nice' to me, I would tolerate his behaviour.

That night, it was a bit chilly in my room. I snuggled down under the covers, ready to go to sleep. I was just about to close my eyes when I heard the "Uncle" enter the room and saw him coming towards my bed. I was wondering what he was doing, but didn't say anything. He climbed into my bed and got underneath the covers with me. Then he said, 'Good girl. Nice girl', and started to touch me. I didn't like it at all, so I asked him "What are you doing?" He replied, "Practising. This is what grown-ups do. We practice." I was confused and asked him, "What are you practising?" He asked me, "Do you like sex?" I had not heard of this before. "What is that?" I asked. He said nothing. After a while, I had enough of him touching me and asked him to leave me alone. Then again he said, "Don't tell your mum. You are a good girl." Yeah, yeah.

Chapter 5: Back to the Past

Stirring It Up Exercise: Are You a Good Girl/Boy?

Take a piece of paper or a notebook and pen to write out the answers to the questions below.

1. What were you told about being a good boy or girl when you were younger?
2. What effect did it have on you at the time?
3. What effect does it have on you now?
4. How would you prefer to see yourself now?
5. How would you prefer to feel about yourself?

Painful Lessons Become a Blessing In Disguise

Even though I did not fully understand what was going on, I somehow knew that it was wrong, otherwise why would the 'Uncle' ask me not to tell my mother? He molested me whenever he had the opportunity, which made me increasingly despondent. After some time, something inside me awoke. It was my Internal Power System, although I did not know this at the time. It told me 'Enough! Stop him!' So one day, as the 'Uncle' was creeping towards me yet again, I pronounced that I did not wish him to touch me ever again. He was taken aback and tried to tell me I was a good girl, but I threatened to tell my mother, which made him finally stop. Unfortunately, the experience with the 'Uncle' and my request for it to stop closed one door, but opened up another even less pleasant one, which I cover in the next chapter.

Today being a mother myself, I realise that one of the greatest gifts you can give your child is a sense of their own self-worth that does not depend on anything outside of them. My daughter Jade is not a good girl or a bad girl based on her behaviour. I am not always thrilled by her behaviour and she knows that too, but my love for her is not based on her behaviour, her looks, her talents or her ability to do homework. Jade is simply someone I love very deeply. She is a part of me and I love that part of me.

The relationship with my parents taught me how important it is as a parent to love your children exactly as they are. In doing so, I hope that Jade will be able to back herself throughout her life in a way that I was not able to back myself in my younger years. Seeing her self-confidence reassures me that she will be able to do so. The relationship I have with Jade is thanks to my parents teaching me this, even though I did not realise it at the time. Thank you, Mum and Dad.

Two years later, at the age of eleven, I learnt what sex was in a biology lesson. At the time, when I remembered the incidents with the 'Uncle' I felt ashamed that it had happened. I started to feel a great bitterness towards him. How could he have tried to carry out adult acts with a child? This also deepened my fear that I was never able to be a good girl, that I was always doing the wrong thing. I know that this was adding further to the deterioration of my spine and the tension in my back. Have you ever had an experience where you felt ashamed? Did you notice what effect that had on your body? How did it feel?

Since then, I have realised that the 'Uncle' was thousands of kilometres away from home and had been looking for love. That may sound strange to you, but people look for love in the strangest of ways. Some people turn to sexual acts as a way of finding love because they do not know any other way. When the 'Uncle's' wife was not available and no other adult female was present, he turned to the next best substitute – me with my naivety and the body of a woman at the age of nine. I became the focus of his attention.

People are very resourceful at filling unmet needs, or voids as they are also called, because these make them feel very uncomfortable. Some sort of action needs to be taken to remove the discomfort. Some people fill the unmet needs or voids by looking for healthy ways to satisfy them. You will find these are people who back themselves in life. Other people use alcohol, drugs, cigarettes, sex and certain behaviours to fill the void. These are people who often do not back themselves in life. The 'Uncle' was using me to fill his void. Looking back now, I learned from him that filling the void in unhealthy ways is never a good solution in the long run. I learned that the only person who can truly value me, love me unconditionally and give me whatever I need, is me. It was a painful lesson to learn at the time, but now I appreciate what I learnt from him. It has helped me to assist my clients and friends who have had challenging experiences in their early years to appreciate what they learnt from them.

Chapter 5: Back to the Past

Hey! I Know It All Already

Because I was so developed, the other children at school, especially the girls, would laugh at me at times because I was so different to what is 'normal'. A nine-year-old girl with breasts was totally weird. When they said something demeaning to me, it was not much better or worse than what I told myself anyway. Well, it was my fault for being so ugly, or fat, or stupid, or selfish or a combination of these. Wasn't it? At other times, if any of the girls at school said something nice to me, I would brush it off because my programmed belief of "I am not good enough" would come into play.

I was prepared to deal with anything that was thrown at me because I knew it all already. I already knew how worthless I was. It was an extremely lonely time in my life. At home, I was with parents who I felt did not love me and at school I was with children who laughed at me. The belief that I was not worth anything became more deeply ingrained. I was a freak, a misfit, someone who could never do anything right, someone who was not worthy of love. This formed within me a deep fear that something bad was bound to happen to me for being such an awful person. As the priest back in Goa had said – your sins are never forgotten. My sin of being an awful person had to be punished. This belief left the door wide open for the next chapter in my life.

Based on my childhood experiences, I became a world-class champion in self-judgement. I would put myself down before anyone else did. It was a great defence mechanism because before anyone else could say something negative to me I had already done it. No nasty surprises left! This self-judgement caused me frequent bouts of depression. My emotions would yo-yo up and down. My natural tendency towards joy would put me on a high at times, only to then experience a big crash at the smallest sign of something not going the way I expected or someone not behaving the way I expected. I started to believe that these things were happening as a punishment for me and it made me fearful. This judgement was like a poison, causing me to dislike myself and often to be angry with other people. I did not enjoy being like that, but I also did not know what to do about it. Reflecting back now, I realise that the self-judgement started to become less and less strong the more and more I was able to love and accept myself later in life.

Unleashing Exercise: Blast Through Your Fear!

This exercise, based on *The Work* by Byron Katie and NLP, consists of questions and a process to change beliefs which Ben Harvey created. It is perfect for loosening the hold that fear has on your mind. Take a piece of paper or a notebook and a pen. Write out the answers for all the following points.

1. Write down a fear you currently have. Give it a score out of 10 where 1 means the fear is hardly there and 10 means it is pretty strong.
2. Is it true?
3. How do you know?
4. Are you absolutely sure it is true?
5. What is it costing you to hold on to this fear? Make a list of the costs in non-financial and also financial terms if applicable.
6. What will it cost you to hold on to this fear in the next 10-15 years?
7. What benefit are you getting by holding on to it?
8. What would you be like without it?
9. Write out the total opposite of the fear.
10. Check how strong that old fear is now on a scale of 1 to 10.
11. How do you feel about that old fear now?

Facing your fears is a great way to weaken and dissolve them. Fear thrives on being hidden in a dark corner so when you shine a light on it, it loses its strength. Darkness cannot dispel light, but light can dispel darkness. Our past experiences condition us to think, act and react in certain ways. They can also cause us to become fearful. By recognising that this is happening, we can move beyond our past conditioning. Sometimes we have to work hard to let go, but it is definitely worth the effort. When we were younger, we had less control over what happened to us, but that is not the case any longer. As we grow older, we have much more control. We can start now by taking full responsibility for our lives in order to leave the past behind and create a brighter future for ourselves.

Chapter 6: Backing Yourself By Taking Responsibility

"The willingness to accept responsibility for one's own life is the source from which self-respect springs."

Joan Didion

Some people choose to keep the past alive and refuse to take responsibility for their lives going forward. Others prefer to blame other people for their circumstances rather than taking charge of their own lives. My parents were definitely amongst these people. Yet some other people take limited responsibility for their own lives and prefer to hand over power to other people. My mother was one of those people. You will not be surprised to read that my parents did not back themselves in life and so felt helpless, powerless and resentful much of the time. People who are not able to take responsibility for their own lives then often have difficulty taking responsibility for their children.

Theoretically, in society our parents are our caretakers who protect us and teach us the right skills in life so that we can thrive and be healthy, happy human beings. Unfortunately, nobody explained this to *my* parents. On the one hand, they would provide us with our basic needs, but on the other hand, they would then be annoyed about having to do so. They felt that they had not been given the best in life when they were younger and resented the fact that as children my brother Blaise and I "had it so easy".

They protected us from strangers and physical danger outside the home, but at home caused us physical and mental harm if they were in a bad mood or drank too much. When we were happy, they were happy one minute and then the next would resent it. "Why are you so happy? You are so ungrateful," was a comment we often heard from them. They acted as if they had been forced to do the job of being parents without anyone asking them first and were totally surprised, dismayed and angry at what they were expected to do in terms of raising children. As you have probably guessed, it was far from being a 'happy household'.

The Dark Prison of Misery

My parents' Model of the World was that they had a tough upbringing and now the world owed it to them to make their lives easier. This meant that my brother and I were always expected to behave exactly as they wanted or they would turn the full force of their anger and disappointment on us. This view of the world was made worse by the fact that they drank heavily. When they got home from work they reached straight for the bottle of Scotch whisky. They drank even more heavily on the weekend. Growing up in our house meant that you had to tread very, very carefully or you would receive verbal abuse, receive a slap across the face, take a blow to some other part of your body or have your head banged against the wall.

My brother Blaise and I, being pretty resourceful as children are, would use going to school and outside to play as our means of escape. The rest of the time at home, we never quite knew what we were in for. Sometimes, there would be peace and at other times, all hell would break loose, as my parents took out their frustrations about their life on each other and us. I often used to cry myself to sleep, feeling that the world was a bleak and unpleasant place to live.

Still, children are very resourceful and will do whatever they can to try and have fun. One way to do this is to have fantasies. To sum up my childhood, my favourite fantasy for many years was that these were not my real parents. I had been kidnapped and my real parents would come one day and rescue me from these awful people. Of course, this never happened because they were my real parents. But they were both people in a lot of pain, even though I didn't realise it at the time. Their behaviour towards my younger brother, each other and myself was the product of their own internal pain and their upbringing.

They were brought up in a small village in Goa, India and were neighbours. My mother was the fifth of six children and my father had an older brother. Both their fathers had died when they were very young, leaving the mothers to look after the children as best they could. Given that in those days, women rarely had jobs and there was no social security, it was pretty tough. As children, they were often hungry, as there was not enough food to go around. They experienced hardship and a lack of the normal 'luxuries' children take for granted these days, such as regular meals, toys and sweets. This was to stay with them for the rest of their lives.

In Chapter 4, I described how we form our Model of the World. In my parents' world, there was a huge amount of lack, fear and loneliness. In later years, through hard work and consistent saving and investing of the money they earned, they amassed a substantial sum of money. However, even though they lived in an amazing location right in the heart of the West End in London, had plenty of money in the bank and had two children who were doing extremely well for themselves, their 'reality' was still one of lack and hardship. My father continued to recount how he had started work at the age of sixteen and was therefore tired. Of course for him, the tiredness has nothing to do with his drinking half a bottle of whisky, smoking a packet of cigarettes every day and constantly telling himself that he had a hard life.

My mother lived in her past and kept it alive. She often told us about her 'problems' of how she was starving as a child, how she had been abandoned by the man she had really loved and how my father had got her pregnant at a time when pregnancy out of wedlock was a shameful thing. For her, the event of my conception was not her responsibility and was entirely my father's fault. Then came the story of how when she moved into their newly-built home, her mother-in-law seemed to be the boss of the house, which at that time was pretty normal. I have no doubt that my mother experienced hard times and pain. She was in some very difficult situations. However, at some point in your life, you have to let go of the past and be willing to create a new future for yourself. Sadly, she chose to make my father and everybody else including myself responsible for her misery. In her perception of the world, if she had not fallen pregnant with me, she would not have ended up in this situation, married to someone who was not her true love.

If I was singing, my father or mother would get into a rage and ask what I was up to, or start criticising me in some way. If I was excited about going out somewhere, my mother would criticise my appearance until I felt totally flat like a balloon with all the air taken out of it. Every birthday, Easter and Christmas celebration would disintegrate into a mess. My parents would drink way more than usual and then argue with each other. After a while, they would try to drag my brother and myself into the argument. When we refused to be drawn in, there would be more arguments and physical and verbal abuse heaped on us both. It started to make me feel unprotected, unloved and unsafe. It is no wonder that I started to form a dread of feeling happy. As I was growing up, a feeling of happiness was closely followed by something very unpleasant occurring. This created a fear within me of something bad happening to me, which was to stay with me until my mid-forties.

When you feel disempowered in some or several areas of your life as I did, it leaves you open to being mistreated by others. Based on my experiences with my parents up until the age of eleven, I was so disempowered in many ways in my life that what happened next was inevitable.

The 'Nice' Neighbour Corners Me

As I described above, my relationship with my parents when I was a child was not a happy one. My parents were the product of their own painful childhoods and were doing their best to cope with their own pain. They had never learned how to be loving, as they themselves had not experienced loving environments. You cannot give what you do not have.

I did not know any of this at the time though, so my main state as a child was one of fear and my second state was one of confusion. In spite of my best efforts, I always seemed to be getting into trouble and never seemed to do the right thing. My brother was the golden child and as he was the younger one, I was responsible for him. If he did anything "naughty", it was my fault because "You have been teaching him. He learns from you." Really? Like when he gets into fights, I taught him that. How? I never get into fights. It drove me crazy and I felt really angry and bitter. But that is how it was in our household.

I often used to lie in bed, wondering why I was being punished this way. What had I done? Please, someone help me. Please, take me away from these horrible people. Please take me to the people who love me, my grandmother and my Aunt Aby. But no help arrived. There was no one who could possibly back me up. This was because in the bigger picture of life, I was destined to learn to back myself, as we all are. But I did not know this at the time, which left me hungry for love and affection and left me feeling very vulnerable.

At the age of eleven, I was going down the stairs from the flat where we lived on the first floor to the ground floor to play with the neighbouring children. As I did, a neighbour who lived on the third floor passed me. He was in his mid-forties, with dull blue eyes that sat behind his square gold rimmed glasses. He said, "You are beautiful." I stopped. I was astounded. My mother was often telling me I was a freak and that I was like a big buffalo. The girls at school laughed at my appearance, so to hear someone telling me the opposite was a big jolt to my system. He asked, "Can I give you a kiss?" I was not keen on the idea. Kissing on the mouth was a disgusting idea. Yuck! "No. I hate kissing on the mouth." Back came the reply "OK. Just one kiss. I promise." I let him give me a little kiss. It was disgusting. His breath stank of cigarettes and he was *ancient*, forty-four years old! I was at the ripe old age of eleven. Eeee-yuck!

Then he said, "Don't tell your mum. She will just blame you. But I know you are a good girl." How did he know? Just like the 'Uncle', he realised that my parents were less than kind to me and played on that by trying to be 'nice' in a way that suited him. Again, I did not feel that my parents would back me up. If anything, I was afraid that they would accuse me of being the 'bad' person yet again. That one meeting confirmed for the neighbour that I indeed would not tell my parents anything for fear of getting into trouble.

From that first time, he would take any opportunity he could to grab hold of me and molest me. I was paralysed by self-doubt and feelings of worthlessness. I so wanted to be a "good girl"! At home, it seemed I never was. Why did being a "good girl" have to be so unpleasant? Why did I have to be subjected to him touching me when I didn't like it? Why did I have to endure the smell of his cigarette-laden breath? His words would reverberate through my ears: "It's your fault for being beautiful." On the outside, I sighed with resignation. On the inside I screamed. I raged. YES!!!!!! It's my fault. Everything is my fault. I can never get things right! I am worthless! I deserve to be punished. So I resigned myself to the fact that I would have to keep playing this cat-and-mouse game because I didn't deserve any better. This was all I was worth. I believe that around this period in my life, my body started to really turn against itself. I suddenly stopped growing and my spine started to be affected.

Deep inside, I hoped that someone would rescue me. I hoped that someone would notice what was happening and step in to help me. Every so often, another neighbour would be passing by on the way to their apartment, but they always turned a blind eye. No one wanted to get involved. One day, I realised the harsh truth – there was not going to be a rescuer for me. The only person who could rescue me from the clutches of my neighbour was me.

One day, I had come back from school and was on the ground floor of the building where we lived, on my way up to our first floor apartment. As I entered the building, it was cool inside and instantly the stench of stale cigarette smoke hit me. I knew he was there. Waiting for me upstairs. There was a tiny glimmer of hope. Maybe he didn't see me coming into the building. Maybe he would just carry on up the stairs and go into his apartment. My heart started hammering in my chest. I crept and hid under the stairs and was very quiet. No such luck. He called down, "I am still here. I know you're down there." Oh no! How can I get away from him? Luck was on my side. Another neighbour from the top floor of the building came down the stairs and started a conversation with him. I moved my legs as fast as they could carry me and bolted up the stairs, running right past the both of them and let myself into our apartment. I slammed the door shut and locked it behind me. Phew! Well done, me! This is when I realised that I had had enough of the abuse.

Busting Myself out of the Corner

I had reached a point where I did not care anymore whether my parents would blame me or not for what happened. I decided to back myself without anyone's assistance. This was when I 'woke' up. Something inside me, some hidden strength that had never made itself known before, presented itself. It was my Inner Power System. The next time the neighbour tried to touch me, I threatened to tell my mother. He looked at me with his dull blue eyes. "She will just tell you it's your fault." It was as if he had read my thoughts out loud. He was probably right, but I was unwilling to subject myself to any more of the abuse. This newfound strength drove me to tell him, "I don't care. I hate what you have been doing to me." He touched my cheek and said, "Hate is a strong word. I know you don't particularly enjoy it. But it's your fault."

I screamed inwardly. He knew how much I hated what he was doing! But he had been putting me through it anyway. In that moment, I started to question whether it really was my fault. I felt stronger than I had ever done before and stood my ground, threatening to tell my parents if he ever dared to touch me again. I was immensely proud of myself for having my own back in that moment. But I did not realise at the time that after years of feeling guilty about so many things the 'It's your fault' program was already imbedded deep within my subconscious, ready to undermine me at a moment's notice in my adult life. The full reaction to the years of abuse was to come later when I least expected it and undermine my sense of self-worth yet again.

Principle: Everything is Your Responsibility, Nothing is Your Fault

This principle has transformed my life in many ways over the years and continues to do so. When I tell my clients and friends about this principle they are often perplexed. "But how can that be?" they ask me. They then go on to question how on earth they are supposed to be responsible for things that are beyond their control. I totally get where they are coming from. This is how I felt when I first came across this principle. However, there are several aspects of taking responsibility that many people are not aware of.

At the first level, taking personal responsibility means that you hold yourself accountable for your own actions and behaviour without feeling culpable or to blame. It also means that you have a duty to deal with something or have a duty of care towards someone, such as a child. It is about taking a conscious approach to the way you respond to circumstances and events in your life. In agreeing to be accountable for your behaviour, you acknowledge that you are the only person responsible for the choices you make in your life. This creates a tremendous sense of freedom within you. Of course, sometimes things happen that are beyond your control and you do not seem to have a choice in this, but you do have a choice about how you respond – how you think, feel and act regarding what has happened. When you realise this, you will feel a sense of your own personal power within you.

At another level, it is important to note that you take personal responsibility for yourself and your own behaviour, not the behaviour and actions of others. Others need to take responsibility for themselves unless they are young children or somehow incapacitated due to, for example, illness. This can be tough because we are conditioned to feel guilty about our actions and behaviours from a young age. "You are a bad girl for not playing with your brother. You are a bad boy for not helping Mummy."

By accepting responsibility for yourself and your responses, you gain a sense of empowerment. It gives you a tremendous sense of freedom to create life the way you want it. By contrast, when you refuse to accept responsibility for yourself and your responses and blame others or circumstances, you disempower yourself. Blaming others or blaming events makes you feel powerless and creates feelings of anger and resentment. Does this sound familiar to you? My father was often angry and resentful as he refused to take responsibility and preferred to give excuses for his behaviour and actions. He would then turn to alcohol, cigarettes and physical abuse of his children to numb the pain of his past and his present circumstances, which were not the way he wanted them to be. His favourite excuse for not making changes to his life was, "You can't teach an old dog new tricks."

The feeling that you have no control over your life can also lead to depression and anxiety. My mother often experienced this as she refused to take responsibility, so she ended up feeling like she had no control over her life. Life was something that happened to her. She would also turn to alcohol and began physically and mentally abusing her children to numb the pain.

As a child you do not know enough about the world in order to take responsibility for yourself so you rely on the adults in your life to help you. In my case, the adults in my life had no idea how to do this for themselves let alone act as a guide for a developing child. I formed the belief that everything was my fault because that is what I was often being told. So I took on responsibility for the actions of other people, which was not mine to take. For example, I started to believe that if my brother misbehaved, it was my fault. If my parents hit me, it was because I had made them do it. When the neighbour abused me, he told me that what was happening was my fault because I was beautiful. Obviously, now it is clear that none of this was my fault but at the time I felt responsible and culpable, which was very unhealthy for my well-being.

Over the years a common situation I have seen is as follows. One of my clients told me how overwhelmed she was by the amount of work she had to do. It was exhausting her. When I asked her what she had done to ease her workload the answer came back, "I try to get as much done as I can but my boss keeps giving me more work. He doesn't seem to realise how much I have on my plate". When I asked her, "Have you told your boss that you are overloaded right now?" The answer was along the lines of, "No. He is my boss so he should know." When I asked, "So does your boss closely monitor every single task you do each day?" The answer was also, "No".

So the first thing she did was to have a conversation with her manager about her workload. It turned out that he had been totally unaware of the situation. He had been expecting that each person in the team would take responsibility for themselves and signal when they had too much to do. When no one said anything he passed on more work thinking everything was fine. It was the responsibility of my client to inform her manager when she was overloaded and ask for assistance instead of assuming her manager knew. Once she did so, he was able to get extra assistance for her and also delegate some of the work to a different person. She ended up with a much more manageable workload and regained her energy.

Another one of my clients took on responsibility for other people instead of letting them take responsibility for themselves. She shared with me that friends would come and talk to her about their issues and their lives. She would then try to fix their problems and often felt drained by it. I helped her to understand that the reason she felt drained was that she was taking responsibility for her friends and trying to fix their problems for them. She recognised that she needed to let them take responsibility for themselves. By doing this, she stopped being drained and quickly regained the energy she had lost.

Someone who takes responsibility for themselves does not blame other people for things that are not working in their life. Unfortunately, many people respond by blaming someone else for their problems or their situation. They shift their own responsibility onto someone else, and then judge the other person for failing to perform as expected! From conducting research on the Internet and personal observation, here are some common traits of people who accept full responsibility in their lives and feel empowered as a result:

- They do not beat themselves up with negative self-talk
- They remain accountable and do not pass their accountability on to someone else
- They do not give excuses for why they did something or for not doing something
- They acknowledge that they are doing their best

- They accept that some days their best is better than on other days!
- They feel able to choose how to respond to an event, situation or person
- They look for the positive aspects or hidden benefits in any situation
- They accept that they created what they have and where they are at present
- They look to themselves to get them from where they are in life now to where they would rather be

Which of the above statements is true for you?

Stirring It Up Exercise: Taking Responsibility

This exercise is in two parts. The first part is for you to recognise where you are not taking responsibility for something that is your responsibility and the second part is for you to recognise where you are taking responsibility that belongs to someone else. Take a piece of paper or a notebook and a pen to write out the answers to the questions below:

Part A

1. Where in your life are you pointing the finger at someone else and blaming him or her for a particular situation?
2. Where in your life are you avoiding taking responsibility for something because you are too embarrassed or afraid of the consequences?
3. Where in your life are you waiting for someone else to do something and getting annoyed that they are not? What is stopping you doing it?
4. Where in your life are you giving excuses for not taking action?
5. What impact is not taking responsibility having on your life?

Part B

6. Where are you taking responsibility for someone else when they could do this themselves?
7. Have you had someone in your life try to make you take responsibility for his or her actions?
8. Where have you taken responsibility for someone through guilt?

9. How do your answers to questions six, seven and above make you feel?
10. What impact does taking unnecessary responsibility for someone else have on you?
11. What do you want to do about it?

When we do not accept responsibility, we feel less empowered. When we take on responsibility that is not ours, it drains us of energy and also weakens our sense of personal power. It is also detrimental to the person involved as they then end up feeling as if they are not able to help themselves and this lowers their self-esteem. To maintain our sense of personal power, we must accept personal responsibility where it is appropriate and also allow others to take responsibility for themselves instead of trying to do it for them.

Respond with Ability

I have often read that the word responsibility is made up of two words: response-ability. Our ability to respond to situations and events in our lives affects our level of fulfilment in life. In taking on board what the 'Uncle', the neighbour and my parents had told me I went beyond taking responsibility for everything and empowering my life. I completely missed the mark and instead started to blame myself for everything. Shame and its close friend Guilt became my constant companions. I felt ashamed that I mostly got Grades of 'B' and sometimes 'A' instead of only 'A's, I felt ashamed of my body, I felt ashamed that I was ugly, I felt I was boring without a personality. No wonder the girls at school laughed at me. In my Model of the World, everything was wrong with me. I felt guilty about my appearance, my behaviour, not being smart enough, my inability to make friends. It was all my fault. This caused me to become very fearful of life. As I mentioned in Chapter 4, this fear started to eat away at my body, impacting my spine and back.

I used to wonder what it would be like if I was dead. Maybe that would be better for everyone and certainly less painful for me. Then I remembered the images of hell the priest had shown the children back in Goa. Committing suicide was one of the worst sins. If you did this, you had no hope of entering heaven, you were destined to go straight to hell. 'Oh, great!' I thought. I can't even escape to somewhere better through death. So I resigned myself to going through the motions of life all the while feeling like I had already died.

To cope with life some people will resort to using substances such as cigarettes, drugs, alcohol, chocolate or other food. Other people will resort to certain behaviours: sexual acts, compulsive cleaning, obsession with order and other behaviour patterns. My neighbour resorted to his behaviour with children in order to help himself feel better about his own life. It is clear that he did not have his own back so he did not know another way and he had no one to assist him with finding one. In my own life, I have often resorted to alcohol or foods with sugar in order to numb myself when life felt tough until I learnt more empowering behaviours.

I am going to ask you a question. Before you answer, promise yourself that you will not feel shame or guilt about the answer. Remind yourself that you are doing your best at any given moment. In some moments, your best is better than in other moments, depending on what is going on in your life. Question: What addictions are you aware of that you turn to when you need comfort or are finding life difficult? How do you feel about doing that? Rather than feeling shame or guilt, recognize that these are your coping mechanisms. If you are not happy with them, it is a pointer that says, "Time to find something better or healthier!!" By backing yourself in this way through kindness towards yourself, you will find it much easier to work towards adopting a new behaviour. Looking back now, I realise that my neighbour had needed assistance with his behaviour with children. However, there was none available for him and he probably never even thought to seek assistance. Although for much of my life, I felt that he caused me pain, I now realise he was also one of my greatest teachers in life.

What I Learned From the Neighbour

Some of the key things I learned from the neighbour are:

- When you feel at your lowest, your Inner Power System is there to help you through it. However, you need to be willing to listen to it.
- Tough experiences can make you stronger and help you dig deeper inside yourself to build your resilience.
- When you can forgive someone who has put you through pain, you free yourself from the past and create a brighter future for yourself.
- My neighbour's inability to take responsibility for himself created a big void within him that needed to be filled with something.

- It is essential to care for and nurture children in their early life so that they gain a strong sense of who they are. This has helped me to be a more conscious parent for my daughter Jade. I want to ensure that she does not have to live through similar experiences to mine.
- Everyone is doing the best they can at any given moment in time and with the resources they have available. If you are in pain, which is either physical or emotional, it has an adverse effect on your behaviour. If your Model of the World is of an uncaring world, you are hardly likely to behave in a loving and caring way towards others. Looking back now, I realise that my neighbour was in a lot of pain.

The Impact of Being Over-Responsible

Previously, I wrote that when you take on responsibility that does not lie with you, this means you are being over-responsible. It is draining. On the other hand, when you respond with ability you free up more of your personal power and you regain your energy as the following story shows.

Two female clients each found themselves in a situation they were not happy with. Although they had full-time jobs, they ended up doing most of the housework as well. Therefore, they had no time left to exercise and look after themselves better. This was causing them to feel tired and dissatisfied. I asked each of them a simple question, "Who said you have to do that?" One of them asked, "What do you mean? It's expected." The other asked, "Isn't that what you are supposed to do?"

I asked again, "Who said you have to do a full-time job, do all the housework and look after the kids?" They both thought about it briefly before replying, "No one." A light bulb moment occurred. It dawned on each of them that nobody had actually asked or even ordered them to do all the things they were doing. They had taken on the responsibility for others in their household themselves without anyone asking them to do so. This is a common example of being over-responsible. The result was that they ended up being overwhelmed and then became frustrated about it.

The solution was simple: Stop! They had not been backing themselves and sharing the tasks between themselves, their partners and where possible their children. They discussed dividing the tasks with the other members of their families. When the other members of the family started to take up their share of the household tasks, both clients were able to start looking after themselves more and began exercising again. They also felt far less inner tension from having too much to do.

I could write a whole book on why women (and some men) take on board so much responsibility unnecessarily, but this is not the point of the story. The point here is that you often feel obligated to do something without asking "Why am I doing this? Is it really my sole responsibility for doing this? What can I hand over to other people?" When you ask these types of questions and stop taking responsibility for others, you are taking another step towards backing yourself in life.

Unleashing Exercise: Respond with Ability

This exercise is intended to help you respond with ability so that you access more of your personal power! Take a piece of paper or a notebook and a pen. Write out the answers to all the following questions. You can use your answers from the earlier Stirring it Up Exercise: Taking Responsibility for this if you wish. It is in three parts. Parts A and B focus on you and in Part C, the focus is on other people.

Part A

1. Where in your life are you not taking responsibility?
2. What impact is this having on you?
3. What is stopping you from doing so?
4. What would happen if you accepted the responsibility?

Part B

5. Where in your life do you feel like something is your fault?
6. When you look at it ask yourself: Is that really true? Are you 100% sure?
7. How would you feel if you stopped blaming yourself or feeling at fault?
8. When are you going to stop blaming yourself?

Part C

9. Where in your life are you taking on responsibility for other people?

10. What is causing you to do this?
11. How would you feel if you handed the responsibility firmly back to the person/people involved?
12. When are you going to do this?

Taking responsibility for everything in your life is very empowering. It puts you in the position where you are able to create what you want in life.

In doing so, you must stay aware of when you are also taking unnecessary responsibility for others instead of letting them take responsibility for themselves. As I wrote previously, it can disempower people, leaving them feeling as if they are incapable of helping themselves. It is fine to take responsibility for young children, as they are not fully able to do so for themselves until they are older and people who are incapacitated in some way. Letting older children and adults take responsibility for themselves results in them gaining a sense of their own personal power and creates a feeling of fulfilment within them.

Who Has Got *Your* Back?

Chapter 7: Back Your Own Happiness and Fulfilment

"The best years of your life are the ones in which you decide your problems are your own. You do not blame them on your mother, the ecology, or the president. You realize that you control your own destiny."

Albert Ellis

As I described in the previous chapter, my mother and father chose to keep the past alive and live with excuses rather than taking responsibility for their own lives as adults. What neither of them realised was that by insisting on living in their past, they were completely destroying any happiness they could experience in the present moment. Not only that, but they were causing their children to suffer with them. That is, of course, until each child hatched and executed an escape plan! My brother and I used our natural instinct for survival to create a new reality for ourselves. We banded together as a mini army to counteract the dark forces of negativity created by our parents and sought to create light in our own lives so that we could feel fulfilled and happy. Sadly, the mini army could not penetrate through the strong fortress the dark forces had created in order to rescue the parents and also bring them out into the light.

Every so often, we managed to create chinks in the fortress walls, but never managed to demolish the walls completely. We now know that it was not actually our job to dismantle the walls. It was the job of our parents, but our parents sought to stay within their dark fortress, as they felt protected there.

The light was just too frightening for them. Letting the light in would mean they had to change and give up their problems, live in the present moment and actually take responsibility for their own lives and happiness as adults. As I wrote earlier in the book, change is the number one fear we have. So my brother and I continued to work to create a bright world for ourselves while at the same time our parents continued to reside in their dark, gloomy one.

The Escape Plan

My escape plan consisted of moving from home to University to study, so that not only was I physically away, but also through getting a degree in engineering could guarantee employment so I would never have to go back and rely on my parents again. However, this is when I also started to notice the effects of my childhood experiences. I really enjoyed the studies, but they were also really tough at times. I would then begin to doubt myself. Maybe I wasn't smart enough to finish the degree. Maybe I was "a clever girl but stupid at times". Maybe I simply didn't deserve it. However, the prospect of the horror of going back to live with my parents was a great motivator. No matter how low my confidence was, I was determined not to end up back in the hell hole again.

It was during my time at University that I started to notice stiffness in my back and neck. I would often get massages from one of the other students and in my first year, I had a boyfriend who would often massage my neck for me. But no matter how often I got a massage, I would often feel a bit tired and groggy. I just put it down to all the concentrating during lectures and while doing coursework. At that time, I didn't know that the stiffness in my back and neck was because of my spine being twisted and also deteriorating. In addition, I was often stressed about life, which caused the muscles of my back and my neck to become tense and stopped blood flowing properly to my brain. At this stage, I was so used to the uncomfortable feeling that I ignored it and carried on with life. This carried on until I finished university.

A Shadow from the Past Rears Its Head

In my final year at University, I met someone who I ended up being in a relationship with for seven years. While I was with him, the full reaction to my past started to surface in my mid-twenties. Apparently it is normal that early trauma that has not been dealt with starts to surface around this age.

After I had finished my degree, I started living with my boyfriend. He was loving towards me and I felt great at starting this lovely new chapter in my life! However, at times I started to recall what had happened with the 'Uncle' and the 'Nice' neighbour when I was younger. The memories of them touching me made me feel like there were thousands of insects crawling over my body. I felt shame and self-disgust. I would say horrible negative things to myself in an attempt to punish myself for letting this happen to me. This often created the feeling that I just wanted to rip the skin off my body. At these times, I would dig my fingers into my arms and the palms of my hands in order to cause myself pain. It was a way of distracting myself from the maddening thoughts I had and the feeling of my skin crawling.

If my boyfriend was there during those times, he would hold me and make sure I didn't harm myself until the feeling passed. The love and affection he gave me helped me to realise that it wasn't my fault. That what the 'Uncle' and the neighbour had done in molesting me as a child was unacceptable behaviour. Although I believed him on the conscious level, the program "It's your fault" was deeply imbedded in my unconscious mind and seemed to have no erase button! At this underlying level, I had formed the belief that it was somehow my fault.

In Chapter 5, I described how in the earlier stages of our life up to the age of fourteen our critical faculty is not fully developed so as children we are not able to fully discern what our responsibility is. In any case I certainly wasn't able to. So, I took on the words of the adults around me: my mother, my father, my grandmother, the 'Uncle', the neighbour and my school teachers. Because they were adults and they knew better than me, didn't they? After repeatedly being told "It's your fault," my brain created a connection that was hardwired. This meant that whenever anything happened I would automatically feel that it was my fault.

After a time, I found that as I got older, if something went 'wrong' or did not go as expected, I would start telling myself 'It's your fault'. In this way, I learnt to not have my own back and left myself exposed to those seeking to take advantage of others until I reached my early thirties. At this point, two significant events occurred that helped to take my life in another direction at which I started to access more of my personal power.

Uh Oh! Where Did My Back Go?

At the age of thirty, I had started a new consulting job that paid me double the salary of my previous job. I was over the moon! Not only that but I met some wonderful new people, one of whom became a very close friend. One day, I was staying at her apartment in a beautiful area near Richmond in London for an evening of pampering. One of my favourite things in life! She had booked a massage for me with a talented masseuse she knew. The massage was wonderful and exactly what I needed that day. Except I noticed that my neck was still stiff so I asked her if she could massage it for me. She informed me she already had but was happy to do a bit more even though the time was up. After she had finished, my neck felt better, but still not completely relaxed.

Later on, I commented to my friend about this and told her that my neck always felt stiff. She looked at me for a moment and then asked, "Have you ever thought about seeing an osteopath?" I had never heard of one. She explained what they do and that she had been to one for an issue she had with her shoulder. She continued, "My shoulder started feeling better straight away and after a number of sessions it's absolutely fine again." So, I got the details for the osteopath from her and got my first appointment. I did not know what was in store for me.

After collecting my information, the osteopath examined me. He then gently explained that I had several kinks in my spine, which should not normally be there, the spine was skewed to one side and that a vertebra in my neck was sticking out when it shouldn't. Then he asked, "Have you had an accident?" I replied, "Not that I can think of. But I did fall over a lot as a child, so maybe something happened then." He was not sure that would account for what he had found, but said that the osteopathy would be able to help alleviate some of the symptoms such as the tiredness and the fog brain. I could hardly believe it. All these years! So it wasn't the studies or work that had caused the stiffness. My spine had a structural issue. But then came another realisation. "Can you correct the structure?" His reply was non-committal. "It's hard to say. It is possible to correct some of it, but it is not clear to what degree." Oh dear! That's worrying!

Well, at least now I knew what I was facing. So, the routine started being that I would go to the osteopath once every three to four weeks to get treatment. Each time, I felt better as my back and neck were less stiff and I could focus more clearly. It made me feel more powerful in myself. However, after a while I began to feel uneasy at the idea that it was not clear how long this was meant to go on for. I was looking for a cure for my back and it was not clear if there was one. My over-creative mind started all sorts of scenarios of myself in old age: hunched over in agony, unable to move easily and so on. I was wrapped up in this latest fear until something happened that stopped me being so self-absorbed.

The Power of Forgiveness Frees Me from The Past

In early 1999, my father was diagnosed as having cancer of the throat for the second time. He had cancer of the throat for years previously, which the doctors put down to the amount he smoked and drank. He received treatment and the cancer seemed to be 'cured'. They advised him to stop smoking and cut down on the drinking or the cancer would come back. My father agreed. But he used to say, "You can't teach an old dog new tricks." The interpretation I put on this is: "I don't want to change. It is too scary for me." So, he carried on exactly as he had before and the cancer came back.

This time, the doctors operated to surgically remove the cancer. The operation itself was successful, but after years of abuse his liver and kidneys were extremely weak. They stopped functioning so he went into a coma and was put on a life support machine. He could not even breathe on his own so the machine did that for him and was also doing everything else to keep his body going. In the meantime, blood kept seeping out of his body, which then had to be replaced through transfusion. We knew that the chances of him recovering after all the damage he had done to himself were close to zero.

After a few days of my father being on the life support machine, the doctors asked us the difficult question of whether we wanted him to continue like that or whether we wanted them to switch off the machine. There was no doubt in our minds that he was already gone. So we gave the doctors permission to turn off the machine. We were allowed to speak to him. The nurses informed us that even though patients are unconscious, they could still hear us. "So just be aware of that and go ahead and say anything it is that you need to say."

My mother, brother and I were each given time alone with my father in his hospital room. When it came to my turn to be alone with him, I found that the bitterness I had felt for this man for so much of my life had melted away. When

I saw him lying on the bed with all the tubes entering his body, I realised for the first time in my life the finality of death. There were no second chances. There was no coming back. Well, at least not in the same body and in the same way. This was it.

I walked over to the bed and sat on the edge. I took his hand, which was warm, listening to the bleeping sounds of the machines, the smell of antiseptic in my nostrils. I heard my voice saying to him what was in my heart in that moment, "Dad, I forgive you for everything you have ever done. You have been a bastard to me. You have caused me so much misery in my life. But I would never have wished this on you. I would never have wished death upon you. In recent times, things have been so much better between us. I wish it could have all been so different. I wish you the peace you never had in your life. Goodbye, Dad." Then I kissed his cheek.

This was when I had the most incredible experience. It was as if a huge weight had been lifted from me, a weight that I had been carrying around for many years. The resentment and bitterness towards my father that I had been carrying around had been like a huge weight and by forgiving him for everything that had occurred it lifted from me. I immediately felt lighter than I could ever remember. In this moment, I realised the power of forgiveness. It releases you from the past and all negative energy associated with it and launches you into a bright new future full of possibility.

From this moment at the hospital, I noticed that much of the extreme mood swings I had experienced in my life going from feeling good to feeling depressed stopped occurring. They had been caused by the bitterness and resentment, which are like poison for your system. By releasing these feelings through the power of forgiveness, I took a big step forward on the path to healing my life. I realised that there was still a lot of fear that I had yet to deal with and release in order to feel happy and fulfilled in my life. I made a vow that I would do whatever was required. From that moment on, I took full charge of my life.

Afraid of Being Happy

At this point, I find it appropriate to cover a theme that has come up previously – being afraid to be happy. As I was growing up, whenever I felt happy, my mother or my father would get into a bad mood, which would lead to being yelled at, smacked or both. Of course they were doing this as they themselves had not had happy childhoods and found it hard to cope with their children being happy. On the conscious level, they wanted us to be happy, but on an unconscious level, they had a program that made them envious of the happiness of others. Whenever they saw their peers doing well, they were deeply resentful. Even if other members of the family seemed to be doing well in their lives, my parents would find grounds to criticise them out of envy rather than admit that they wanted the same success.

I started to associate being happy with something nasty happening straight after the happy moment. So I spent a large part of my younger life afraid of being happy. In fact, most of my younger life was about fear. I was afraid of doing the wrong thing and being beaten up, afraid of being happy in case it upset my parents, afraid of being molested by the 'Uncle' or the neighbour, afraid of being talked about at school, afraid of getting the best marks and looking like a "girlie swat". This fear prevented me from backing myself in life and also caused the slow deterioration of my upper spine.

As an adult in my twenties and thirties, I experienced moments of happiness, but there was always a sense of unease behind it. Can you relate to this feeling? I had a sense that I could not allow myself to be too happy. If I allowed myself to be too happy, I thought something nasty would happen. Have you ever had this feeling? It is often caused by your experiences as you were growing up where you did not feel safe or supported. Are you aware of experiences in your life which may have led to this feeling?

Not knowing how to deal with the fear, I kept trying to do things in my life that would perhaps help me to feel happy. I had a sense that I was always waiting for something to happen that would make me feel happy.

The Illusion Of "I Will Be Happy When..."

Many people live their lives waiting for something to happen in order to feel fulfilled or experience feelings of happiness. Do you recognise any of the following?

- I will be happy when I find a better paid job.
- I will be happy when I have a new manager.
- I will be happy when my business is more successful.

- I will be happy when I have more clients/customers.
- I will be happy when this is over.
- I will be happy when I meet the right person.
- I will be happy when my partner/mother/father/child stops doing this.
- I will be happy when I lose weight.
- I will be happy when I go on holiday.
- I will be happy when I have more time to myself.
- I will be happy when the kids can look after themselves.

Whenever we are waiting for something like this, we are not backing our own happiness. We imagine how fantastic we will feel when we get a particular outcome in our lives. However, the reality is that when we get the outcome, we only feel fulfilled or happy for a short time. Soon that old feeling of needing more pops us again. So we go after the next thing we believe will give us that feeling of fulfilment and being happy. We put some extra effort in and get the next outcome. Again, we feel fulfilled and happy for a moment but then the old feeling comes back! The more we do this, the more we start to feel that there must be something wrong with us. This was me! My mantra used to be, "What's wrong with me? Why can't I just be happy?"

The reason for this is that we are constantly living in some future moment in time. We have the illusion that something in the future holds the key to our fulfilment and happiness. We rarely take the time to appreciate everything that we already have. In fact, we are actually in fear of losing what we already have! Appreciating and actively enjoying what we have right now keeps us in the present moment. It enables us to feel fulfilled now. It is important to note at this point that feelings of happiness are temporary but feelings of fulfilment are much more enduring.

Unleashing Exercise: Gratitude List

Below is an exercise to help you connect further with your personal power:

Take a piece of paper or a notebook and pen and have fun!

1. Notice how you feel before you begin the exercise.

   On a scale of 1 to 10 where 1 means 'feeling pretty blah' and 10 means 'feeling great', what score would you give yourself?

2. Make a list of all the things that exist in your life that you are grateful for.

   Everything is valid for this list. I myself am grateful for having hot water to shower in every day and clean water to brush my teeth! I am also grateful for the clients I have.

3. Notice how you feel after making the list.

On a scale of 1 to 10, where 1 means 'feeling pretty blah' and 10 means 'feeling great', what score would you give yourself now?

When we are grateful for something, we appreciate it. Feelings of gratitude and appreciation lift our spirits. When you choose to live in gratitude, you are in fact backing your own happiness and fulfilment.

What Are You Waiting For?

Previously, I wrote that many people are waiting for something. You may be one of these people. When I work with clients I notice that at the beginning they are all waiting for something to make them happy. This 'something' is often one of the things I listed in the section titled "The Illusion Of I will be Happy When...". I listen intently and make notes. Over time I work with them to help them realise that what is happening in their external lives is a reflection of what is happening inside them. The time to be happy is now and the only person that can make them happy is themselves. If they are internally dissatisfied with themselves and life, the Universe will just give them more things to be dissatisfied about. If they are internally grateful, the Universe will provide them with more things to be grateful about. So a good place to start is to decide to be happy right now and not wait for something or someone. The gratitude list from the previous exercise is a great tool to help you with this.

That said, sometimes we are actually blocked due to past experiences, as in my case. When this happens, it is extremely useful to notice what sort of emotions or blocks you become aware of and make a note of them – and then work on systematically removing them. If you feel prevented from feeling happy by a belief you have formed about yourself, e.g., "I am not smart enough," ask yourself a simple question: "Is that true?" If the answer is "Yes," then ask yourself: "Am I totally sure it is true?" The answer will nearly always end up being "No." This already starts to weaken the belief, allowing you to entertain the possibility that you are smart. You can also use the questions for beliefs you have formed about someone or something else, e.g., "People don't like me," "My life is so hard." You start to form stories in your head about your life and yourself that prevent you from feeling fulfilled. By dissolving the old story and telling yourself a new more empowering one, you can set yourself on the road to taking charge of your own happiness and sense of fulfilment.

Taking Charge of Happiness and Fulfilment

I don't know if you have noticed, but there seems to have been an awakening in the world. I have noticed in the last few years that more and more of my clients and people I meet are realising that only they have the power to create fulfilment and happiness in their own lives. A good example of this is one of my clients who had spent a lot of her career waiting to be recognised for her efforts. She was in a role where she led a team and there was always a lot to do, and the project goals were often changing, which was causing her a lot of stress. She felt that she would be happy when the management recognised her efforts.

When management did not recognise her efforts, she felt very frustrated and down. When her managers did recognise her efforts she would gain a sense of satisfaction from it but somehow not long afterwards she would feel down again. She was often also saying "Yes" to too many things and then expecting that she would be happy once the work was done. She was not backing herself at all and was always waiting for something to happen.

She started to realise that waiting for other people to back her and also trying to keep people happy by saying "Yes" was causing her to feel low and unhappy on a regular basis. Furthermore, it was affecting her health, causing her to be tired and ill on a regular basis.

She realised that she herself was the only person that could recognise her own efforts and help herself to feel happy and good about her life. During the coaching, she worked with me on appreciating and loving herself more. She started by valuing her own abilities more and judging herself less. She committed herself fully to her personal growth and over the last couple of years, she has backed herself and made some profound changes in her life. She has gone from being employed in a position that caused her a good deal of stress and gave her little satisfaction to running her own business focusing on doing what she loves.

As a result of all the things she has done to back herself in life, her confidence in her capabilities has grown enormously. This has led to people offering her work and people in her life seeking her assistance with various projects they wish to undertake. At the time of writing this book, she has been helping three different people focus on doing what they love and earning money from it. She has decided to further her studies so that she can help people with transitioning from doing something they don't love to something they do. "Teaching people how to fish" is how she refers to it. Rather than waiting for something to happen or someone else to do something, you need to take charge and do the things that help you feel happy and fulfilled. Start now.

Unleashing Exercise: Stop Waiting!

Take a piece of paper or a notebook and a pen. Write out the answers to the following questions. They are designed to stop you waiting and start you taking action to create what you want in life.

1. What are all the things in life that would make you feel happy and fulfilled? Make sure that your answers do not involve waiting for someone else to do something.
2. What is in common between all these things?
3. Which of these things do you already have? What are your biggest fears of getting these things?

4. What are you doing to stand in the way of getting these things?
5. Why are you doing that?
6. How do you feel about that?
7. What would your life be like if you do not get these things?
8. What would your life be like if you do get these things?
9. Do you really want to get them?
10. What is the first small step you can take?

Review your answers to the questions above and notice how you feel. Taking charge of your life gives you a feeling of empowerment and boosts your confidence. When we do not back ourselves in life, we leave our ability to experience fulfilment in our lives up to other people or up to something happening. What we do not realise is that in doing so, we are giving away our personal power to somebody or something outside of ourselves. When we realise that we are the only ones who can create what we want and also learn to appreciate what we already have in our lives, it increases our sense of strength and automatically increases our level of happiness and fulfilment. You've got the power!

Chapter 8: You Have Everything You Need To Back Yourself

"Man is a Universe within himself."

Bob Marley

Which of these beliefs do you hold about yourself? That you are someone who has many talents, abilities and gifts, or that you are someone that seems to have a lot of things missing? So what do I mean by 'things missing'? You may feel that you are not particularly talented or gifted. Maybe you think you will not be successful in your job or in your business because you doubt your abilities. You may think that other people around you are having an easier time than you because they are smarter. You may feel that you don't know enough. Whichever of these examples applies to you, if you believe you have things missing in you it affects your self-esteem and confidence. It can also leave you feeling inferior to other people around you who may seem to possess the talents, abilities and gifts that you think are not present within you.

When you feel like you are inferior in some way to other people you are more likely to subordinate yourself to the opinion and will of others and society. Why? Well, you are not able to fully trust yourself so you experience self-doubt. When you have the perception that you are somehow not good enough you can also form the rather insidious belief that you are not entitled to have your own opinion or to have things the way you want them to be. The result of this is that you hand your power over to others and let them tell you what to do. So what is the reason for this? Well, these superior people know better than you, don't they? So, maybe it's better for them to take over and run things for you. Does this sound familiar to you? How does it make you feel? You will not be surprised to read that I was one of those people that felt there were lots of things missing in me and you have already seen that I often gave away my power to other people. It made me feel terrible at times and resulted in a lot of negative self-talk.

The Pain of Not Paying Attention to My Own Body Signals

Earlier in Chapter 3, I wrote about the principle of 'If you don't pay attention, you pay with pain'. When I was in my late twenties, I noticed that my back had started to make clicking noises. Often when I moved my back to stretch it, the vertebrae would make a cracking type of noise a lot like when someone cracks their knuckles. This was not pleasant to listen to for anyone around me, and it also concerned me, so I decided to visit our family doctor at some stage. Then one day, I discovered that my menstrual cycle had stopped. This was obviously worrying in someone of my age, so I made an appointment with the family doctor to talk about my monthly cycle stopping and also my back. He was an elderly gentleman, and what I appreciated about him the most was that he very rarely prescribed medication unless it was strictly necessary and no other alternatives were available.

As I entered his office, I felt nervous about what he might find. I was fearful of him finding something life-threatening was wrong with me. I had images in my head of him telling me that I didn't have long to live, or that I would be in a wheelchair for the rest of my life or my birthday must be wrong and I was really fifty not twenty-eight or…Yes. I have a pretty active imagination! After listening to my two main concerns he said, 'Well, before we worry about "click-y" backs let's find out what is happening with your menstrual cycle'. So he did some tests on me and came back with the cure. "Eat more!" he advised. "You are underweight and that is putting your body under stress. A few extra slices of bread each day and you should be fine." I was relieved.

"So what about my back then? What do I do about that?" I asked. He asked whether I was in pain and when I replied that I wasn't, he came back with, "Then just do some regular stretching. There is nothing to worry about." This time I wasn't so reassured, but he was the doctor, wasn't he? He had many years' experience. What did I know? I had no medical knowledge. So I decided to subordinate myself to his superior knowledge. I ate the extra slices of bread as suggested and put on some weight and my menstrual cycle started again. This was great for solving that issue, but did absolutely nothing to help my back.

Even though I started to do the stretches, he suggested the tension never completely went away. I was often tired and feeling fog-brained. This time, I put it down to the type of work I was doing. I was also living with my brother Blaise at the time. On weekends, we would often massage each other's necks and shoulders to release tension from the week. I remarked to him one day that the stiffness I felt in my neck and shoulders may actually be connected with my back making the clicking sounds. His response was, "Chris, you are so used to massages that if you don't have one, your neck and shoulders feel stiff. It's more of a habit." At that time, I admired his intelligence and intellect, feeling that it was superior to mine. Earlier, I wrote that Blaise normally backed me a lot and was also my biggest fan, so I accepted his opinion. Even though I was not totally convinced that he was right, I decided to subordinate my opinion to his.

Two years later, I went to another doctor close to where I was living, as my back, shoulders and neck by then had started to feel progressively worse. This doctor asked how often I stretched and when I replied that I did it regularly he decided to show me more effective stretches. I asked him, "What about the fact that my back keeps making these clicking noises?" "Does it hurt?" "No". His response was, "Then there is nothing to worry about." Ok... so I guess that's it then.

It seemed to me that the general opinion was that I was worrying about nothing. At the time, instead of paying attention to the signals my body was very clearly sending me I chose to listen to other people who were presumably 'experts'. So I ignored the signals from my own body and subordinated myself to the superior knowledge of others. After all, who was I with my lowly bachelor's degree and master's degree to doubt the expert opinion of medical doctors with years of experience? Why did I do this? Due to a lack of belief in myself. At that time I believed that there were many things 'wrong' with me and that I had a lot of things missing in terms of character and abilities.

Ignoring what my own body had very clearly been telling me for years and choosing to subordinate my opinion to the opinions of others worked to my detriment. It meant that I did not begin work on healing my back at all earlier on in my life and so my back became progressively worse. Later in life, I paid a price for not paying attention. I started to experience the discomfort I wrote about in earlier chapters, which as you have read was debilitating at times. Fortunately for me I did eventually put myself on the path to healing, otherwise I dread to think what my life would have ended up being like.

Not paying attention does not have to relate to something physical. It can relate to any area of your life that is not working for you the way you want. What in your life are you not paying attention to? What is making you do this? What impact is it having on you?

Oh Dear, What Can The Matter Be?

This persistent feeling that there were lots of things wrong with me, that I somehow wasn't good enough, persisted for many years. I had a lot of false beliefs about my lack of ability, my lack of skills, my crappy personality, my awful body and my overall appearance. In short, lots of things were 'missing' and I desperately wanted to find something to fill the gap.

But why did I even have this feeling? It came from what I had learned as I was growing up. In Chapter 5 I wrote about the Model of the World that we all form for ourselves. When we are growing up and all through life we are taught to rely on the opinions of others and are also led to believe that we need to rely on the outside world. We look to someone or something outside of us to provide us with love, reassurance, acceptance, approval and more.

When we are very young, from birth up until the age of five, we certainly need to rely heavily on our parents and other adults. As we grow older we are able to do more and more for ourselves. However, at this time we are very rarely encouraged to look within ourselves to see what we already have and are also not taught how to tap into this in order to create a fulfilling life for ourselves. Instead we are taught to see our 'faults' and to judge ourselves. By the time we are adults we are already experts at doing this and end up feeling unfulfilled and unhappy about ourselves and in aspects of our life.

Stirring It Up Exercise: Who Runs Your Life?

1. Do you seek the opinion of others before making a decision?
2. Do you have times when you look to others for approval before or after taking action?
3. Do you look to get attention from others and feel unhappy if you don't get it?
4. Do you need reassurance from others that you are doing the right thing?
5. Do you make a decision and then doubt yourself?
6. Do you regularly seek praise and approval from others?
7. Do you know what causes you to do any of the above?

How many questions did you answer "Yes" to? For a large part of my life, the answer was a constant "Yes" to all of the questions above. My childhood training had been so thorough that I believed there were lots of things missing in me so I couldn't trust myself and had to rely on other people to make decisions for me or to get approval from them.

A Massive Investment In Myself Pays Off

It was when I did a Neuro-linguistic Programming (NLP) Practitioner course at the end of 2007 that I finally started to shift that perception forever. There are many explanations of what NLP is. My personal take on NLP is that it is all about you and how you operate in the world. You start to understand how you became who you are today and the things that influenced you. You understand why you think and behave the way you do. This understanding of yourself can then be applied to other people, too. Having this sort of insight enables you to relate much better to other people because you are able to recognise why they are the way they are. NLP also enables you to change the thought and behaviour patterns that don't serve you. It enables you to become empowered in your own life and help others do the same.

Since I had first heard of NLP, I had a great desire to do a course in order to create changes within myself and also as part of my endeavour to become a highly effective coach. I heard about a package involving learning about NLP and how to apply it in different aspects of your life and the life of others. I was excited!

There was one big drawback, however – the total cost was going to be over twenty-five thousand dollars. Eiko was aghast. "Chris, that is a lot of money! We could use that money for so many other things." I also felt nervous about investing such a substantial amount of money. But my Inner Power System spoke out loud and clear, 'You have never invested in yourself like this before. Look at what this has cost you so far. You are not living the life you truly want and are often feeling bad about yourself. How many more years of your life do you want to spend like this?' In that moment I decided to back myself like never before.

I told Eiko that I wished to invest in myself on a personal level and pointed out that everything I learned would also help me on a professional level, enabling me to offer my clients more value and earn more money as a result. Eiko was not thrilled about parting with such a large sum of money until I said to him, "I don't want to be a good coach. I want to be an excellent coach. I don't want to be like some of those therapists where you go to them for months and years and make little progress. I want to help people move forward in their lives as quickly as possible. These courses will help me to do that. I am convinced we will get the money back through the coaching." He finally agreed and I paid for everything as quickly as possible before either of us could change our minds!

Have you ever been in a situation where you knew you wanted something that would help you in the future but were not sure about the cost? What did you do? How do you feel about the decision now? I am deeply grateful to myself for having moved past my trepidation and made the investment. Since then, not only have I experienced a profound change within myself, but I have also helped clients move past issues they have had for years within the space of a few weeks and often within just one session. For me, this is priceless. I explain more about why NLP works so quickly in the following section.

Rewiring My Own Mind

The first most profoundly useful thing I learned was about the unconscious mind. The conscious mind that we are aware of is estimated to only make up about ten percent of our whole mind. The other ninety percent is made up of the unconscious mind. It is the unconscious mind that drives nearly all of our behaviour but we are not aware of it.

As I described in Chapter 5, we have Developmental Stages in our lives between being born and becoming an adult. During these stages we form connections between the neurons in our brain. These connections are like wiring which speeds up our response to what is happening around us. So, rather than having to think about something for a long time, we respond instantly. A good example of this is that for many years we have been programmed to stop at a red traffic light, so when we are driving and see one we don't have to think about stopping, we are already using the brake. Our response is automatic, as we are not even thinking about it. This type of response is stored in the unconscious mind.

In the same way, if we were told things about ourselves when we were younger, such as "You are so stupid," on a regular basis because we were doing something that our parents were not happy about, our brain would develop a connection or wiring that says "I am so stupid". This means that later on in life whenever you do something that you or someone else is not happy about you will automatically think, "I am so stupid." You will often realise *what* you are doing but not be aware of *why* you are doing it. Again, this type of response is automatic because it is stored in the unconscious mind.

I felt such incredible joy in at last knowing why I kept behaving in ways that did not serve me! Up until that point whenever I tried to change my behaviour, thought patterns or emotions I had struggled and often not succeeded. Then I had felt frustrated with myself for not being able to make the changes and beat myself up for being so useless. The insight regarding the unconscious mind and the way that your brain 'wires' itself gave me a tremendous sense of relief. I realised where I needed to do the work. Not in trying to force myself or beat myself up into changing. I had to change the unconscious patterns that were not working for me into something that was far more beneficial. *Great! There is nothing wrong with me! I am not useless! I do not have anything missing which is preventing me from making changes!*

The NLP course taught me how to form new connections in my brain so that instead of reacting in the same negative way I had for years to many things, I had new and much more positive reactions to anything that occurred in my life.

Principle: Be at Cause in Your Life

Another key concept I learned about on the NLP course was Cause and Effect. My word! It was such a wake up call for me! On the first day of the course the trainer put the following equation up on a flipchart: Cause => Effect. Cause is the action you take or perform which then leads to the outcome or effect of that action. This means that Cause is the key or main action while Effect is the result of this action. The trainer explained that if you lived on the Effect side of the equation life happened to you. On this side of the equation, you live in a reactive mode. You are likely to blame other people such as your partner, your parents, your colleagues or external events for what is happening in your life. The trainer pointed out that you then justify your moods or where you are in life by pointing the finger at other people or external events. Oh dear! I was definitely doing this in my life at the time!

Apparently people living on the effect side of the equation believed that 'If only I was more supported by my partner, my boss, my parents, my friends I would have a much better life'. Whoops! I was also doing that! But coming from this position where you make other people responsible for your results in life or the quality of your life, it actually reduces your personal power. When you are waiting for someone else to do something or something else to happen in order to create a life you love it leaves you powerless and creates pain in your life. Oh wow! At that point in my life, I was definitely living on the Effect side of the equation a lot of the time. I felt like this training course had been especially written for me to help me change my life for the better!

The trainer explained that if you live on the Cause side of the equation you take responsibility and hold yourself accountable for everything that happens in your life. Being at Cause means that you decide what you want to create in life and take the appropriate action to make it a reality. You are not waiting for someone else or something else in order to make your dreams come true. This side of the equation leads to you getting the results you want in life. On this side of the equation, you live in a proactive mode. This means that you take the appropriate action to make things happen and if things are not working you look at other options. On this side of the equation there are choices available to you.

Which side of the equation are you on in your life right now? How do you feel about the idea of being at Cause in your life and taking responsibility for everything in it? You may feel empowered by it or indignant. If you feel indignant, maybe it's because you can see examples in your life where you think, 'Well, that definitely isn't down to me', or 'I don't have control over that', or even 'But someone else did that'. Thoughts of this kind may make you feel better in the short term. However, how do you feel when you constantly respond like this? My guess is that you feel a little or very helpless and that you feel you have no ability to change what is occurring and have things the way you want them to be. In this situation, you are on the Effect side of the equation.

Now let's pretend that you cause everything in your life to occur. You are responsible for it and you have control over what happens. How does that make you feel? My guess is that you feel strong and have a sense of taking charge of your own life.

The trainer asked the group which side of the equation they felt they were on. A light bulb lit up in my head. Oh my word! I realised in a flash that I had spent a large part of my life on the Effect side of the equation. At times, I was still acting like the victim in my life. I was still carrying around my story of all the stuff that had happened to me. No wonder I was so fearful. No wonder I was often worried about my back, money, losing friends, being a bad parent, being a bad wife, being a bad friend and so on. I was not living as someone who is empowered in their life.

In that moment I made the internal decision that from now on I wanted to live on the Cause side of the equation. I wanted to take charge of the health of my back, my emotions and my life. I noticed an energy welling up inside me, a sense of power and an excitement. 'Finally!' I thought, to myself. 'Finally. I am going to learn how to get rid of my baggage from the past once and for all and create a better future for myself!'

One of my clients also benefited from this new knowledge about Cause and Effect soon after I did the course. She was having some issues in the relationship with her husband and also struggling with life. Her husband worked on projects and the days were sometimes long. They had two young children and she had decided that she wished to stay at home with them until they got to school age and she also wished to study something new so that she could find more interesting work later on. It was all too much for her.

She related to me that she found looking after the children and studying hard going. Additionally, her husband would come home and sit on the sofa and did not play with the children at all. She felt that he ought to be spending more time with them when he got home. He also did not ask about her day and she felt as if he were taking her for granted and did not care about all the effort she was putting in to look after the children and the house, and also to study. She would then get upset with him. She had put herself on the Effect side of the equation – life was happening to her.

I explained the concept of Cause and Effect to her and asked her which side of the equation she was on in this situation. She realised immediately that she had put herself on the Effect side of the equation, blaming, accusing and feeling hard done by. So, I helped her to come up with a strategy to bring harmony back into the household. First of all, she realised that it had been her decision to keep the children at home full-time and also her decision to study. Her husband was happy for them to go to day-care. She had the power to make changes if she wished. As a result, she decided to put the children in day-care on two days of the week so that she could study on those days. This immediately took a lot of the pressure off her.

Secondly, she spoke with her husband about the situation. He explained that he really needed some down-time after a hectic day when he first came in and found it hard when she and the children threw themselves at him. So they agreed between them that she and the children would leave him alone when he got home for as long as he needed to enable him to relax. He found that after having this time he was happy to play with the children and he was also more interested in her day. Having taken responsibility for what was happening in her life, my client had firmly put herself on the Cause side of the equation and got the result she wanted – a more harmonious household!

Stirring It Up Exercise: Your Unconscious Patterns

1. What unconscious patterns are you aware of within you that do not serve you?

These will be behaviours that you keep repeating even though they are unhelpful. They will also be thoughts that you keep having and find it hard to stop. They will also be adverse reactions to things you have no control over.

2. What impact is this having on your life?
3. Are you aware of where they came from?
4. What would you be like if you let go of them?
5. What would you need in order to let go of them?

You already have everything you need inside of you to make changes. All you need are some useful techniques!

The Emergence of a New Me!

The first part of the NLP course lasted a whole week, during which I learned to let go of the old me in a big way. During the week, I learned a lot techniques for changing unconscious patterns. For each technique I had the opportunity to be both the coach and the client. By the end of the week, I had dissolved a lot of the unconscious stuff that had been getting in my way my whole life and helped other people on the course to do the same. It changed my entire way of how I viewed myself, others and the world. I found myself moving well and truly towards the Cause side of the equation! This is also where I met the lovely Martine Casagrande, who encouraged me to write this book!

By the end of this first part of the NLP package, I felt empowered in a way I had never felt in my entire life. I was not the only one. The whole group experienced a huge shift in their way of being as each person released a lot of patterns that had been holding them back in life. On the last day of the course, the vibe in the room was incredible. Forty-odd people feeling empowered created such a tremendously strong energy that it felt as if we were going to blow the roof off the building!

For months afterward, I experienced a joy that had evaded me for most of my life. The joy of knowing that there was nothing wrong with me! A joy which has remained with me up until today. Eight months later, I did the Master Practitioner course, which built further on what I had already learned. After this second course, I found myself actually living the principles I had learned. The way I thought and felt about myself had completely changed. Many of my old 'programs' from my upbringing were no longer there.

I used what I had learned on the courses with my clients. The changes in them were incredible! In a very short time, I was able to help them change the way they thought from being pessimistic to optimistic, from being self-deprecating to being self-appreciative and from feeling stuck to feeling like they had options available.

The NLP courses helped me to release a lot of my internal blocks. Following the courses I used what I had learned to move myself on even further and let go of yet more beliefs, behaviours and emotions that prevented me from enjoying my life. In addition, every time I coached my clients and used some of the NLP techniques with them, I also benefitted from what they learned. From everything I had learned to date I had started to understand that all my life experiences had formed me into the person that I am today. Without them, I would not have been able to help so many people. I had reached a stage where a lot of the issues on the surface had been worked on and I was then aware of some deeper underlying patterns which I did not know how to reach. I needed a way to access these deeper layers and got it from a totally unique course.

On the very last course of the NLP Package, I met Benjamin J. Harvey, who as I mentioned earlier in Chapter 4 became my coach and mentor for a time. Through this relationship with him, I came to learn about an amazing course he runs called Unlocking the Freedom Code (UFC). In the years following my doing the NLP package I noticed that at times I still felt uneasy when I experienced feelings of happiness. In spite of my having dissolved many limiting beliefs about myself and life, there was still something else that was blocking me. I felt that this block or these blocks were at a much deeper level than the others I had removed so far.

When I heard about the UFC course from Ben, I just knew straight away that it would help me to free myself of some of this deep conditioning from the past. Additionally, Ben is a great sales guy. When he mentioned that not only would

Chapter 8: You Have Everything You Need To Back Yourself

I free my own blocks, but that I would also be able to help my clients to do the same immediately following the course, I was completely sold on attending it even though it was in Sydney and we were still living in Melbourne at the time. As you may have guessed, I get a real buzz from using powerful techniques. Effective and fast-working healing techniques are a definite obsession for me and I am forever on the hunt for the latest and greatest techniques out there.

When I told Eiko about the course he rolled his eyes at me. "What, another course?" he asked. "Can't you wait until he runs it here in Melbourne?" I ignored him. However, I thought it wise not to spend more money than was necessary in order to attend the course. Gaining new knowledge and losing a husband in the process was not the outcome I was looking for! Have you noticed how when you really want something you become super resourceful and find ways to get it? Or rather the Universe lends you a hand in getting it?

In order to attend the UFC course, I managed to get a substantial discount from Ben, I booked my flights using frequent flyer points and I arranged to stay with friends in Sydney so I did not need to pay for accommodation. I spent the bare minimum possible, which left Eiko with nothing to complain about. Phew! Well done, awesome me!

Attending the course proved to be one of the best decisions I have ever made, as it added a further depth to my understanding that there is nothing missing in us, that we have everything we need inside of us already. I cover the wonderful insights I gained from this course in the following paragraphs and the incredible impact it had on me and the lives of my clients.

Unlocking the Secrets of the Freedom Code

When we learn to love ourselves exactly as we are, even with our 'faults', then in this moment we see that there is nothing missing. This was brought home to me even further from attending Unlocking the Freedom Code (UFC). Earlier, I wrote about the connections that form between the neurons in our brain, the wiring. When we experience events that make a big impact on us, the connections or pathways in our brain become 'blocked'. If an event is perceived as being negative it creates a negative charge and if an event is perceived as being positive it creates a positive charge. In either case this causes the particular pathway in our brain to become blocked or locked and it needs to be unlocked. For example, if you go to a café and have the best hot drink you have ever had in your life, a positive charge will occur. Every time you go to a café, you will then be looking for the hot drink to taste exactly the same and when it doesn't, you will be very disappointed. This block prevents you from enjoying that hot drink again.

An example of a negative charge is illustrated by one of my clients who experienced an event at work where she was criticised by the project manager in front of her colleagues, which made her feel totally disempowered. One of the pathways in her brain regarding work became blocked, leaving her feeling that she was incapable no matter what type of work she was doing until we unlocked it together. These blocks can cause you to feel as if there is something missing in you. They additionally contribute to you judging yourself harshly and also those around you. The thing that holds you back is that you are not able to 'see' yourself clearly as an amazing being. You are 'blinded', so to speak, by these blocks.

During the course, I came to realise for the first time the huge amount of work I had already done on myself. I had already uncovered so much of my personal power. Now, I was ready to do an even deeper excavation. Well, there is no limit to what we have inside us! You can spend your life finding more and more buried treasure inside you! I was not disappointed. The UFC course focuses on helping you to eliminate these deeper hidden or supressed blocks which are stopping you loving yourself exactly as you are and also from achieving what you want in your life and following your purpose.

During the first part of the course, Ben covers the neurological and physiological workings behind your thoughts and emotions to a greater depth than I had ever come across before. This was very helpful in giving me an understanding of what was happening inside my mind. Then during the second half of the course he takes you on a journey which is more to do with connecting with yourself. Ben has developed The Universal Freedom Technique, which he uses to help you unlock blocked pathways in your brain. You spend a good deal of time using the technique to unlock the locked pathways, neutralise old behaviour and thought patterns that are detrimental to your life and replace them with new more empowering patterns.

For myself, I gained a whole new understanding about some of the most traumatic incidents in my life, which had led me to forming beliefs and making decisions about myself and life that disempowered me at a deep level. These blocks added together had created my old fear of something going wrong and had many times prevented me from living in the present moment and feeling good in myself until I did the NLP course package. You will recall that at the end of the series of courses, I felt that there was nothing wrong with me and felt amazing. However, I noticed that at times I still had a slight underlying fear of something about to go wrong or something bad about to happen which I could not get rid of.

During the UFC course, I unlocked locked pathways in my brain which I had never dealt with before. You can imagine how incredibly powerful this was! I began to see even more of who I really am and to truly appreciate all sides of myself like never before. I could also see that many of the events of my childhood which I have written about earlier had a greater purpose in my life. I could see that these events and many others had taught me how to be stronger, more resilient and more compassionate towards others. The events had also taught me how to relate to others, and helped me become a better teacher and more insightful, intuitive coach. I was not alone in this. All the participants gained powerful insights into themselves.

At the end of the course I noticed how much lighter my entire being felt. My body felt stronger. I also gained an even deeper sense of the fact that we have nothing missing in us. We already have everything we need to create the type of life we want. I felt free! This in itself was wonderful. Then I experienced the sheer magic of what had happened even more in the following weeks.

My Personal Key to Freedom

As I stated earlier, the UFC course was run in Sydney and at the time of doing the course in November 2011, I was still living in Melbourne. As I was returning to Melbourne from the course, I felt expanded and free in a way I never have before. The feeling was even stronger than when I did the NLP course package. I felt ready to take on anything! I noticed that the constant feeling of fear I had for many years of something bad happening had finally disappeared forever. Hooray! There are not enough words to describe the deeply profound gratitude I felt and still feel that this happened. For the first time in my life, I felt able to embrace my own wisdom and trust my Inner Power System like never before. Best of all, I felt freer in my life than ever before and more at peace with myself! This meant that I was able to pursue the things I deeply desired without the feeling of fear constantly getting in the way. I was totally ready to back myself in life like never before. No wonder the course is titled Unlocking the Freedom Code!

Of course, since doing the UFC course, I have used the Universal Freedom Technique on a number of clients with wonderful results. It is one of the most powerful ways I have ever come across for helping people to let go of blocks and limitations from the past. It is definitely one of my favourite healing tools.

The first thing I did upon my return to Melbourne was to plan the move to Sydney with Eiko that I described in Chapter 4. Although this move had already been decided before I attended the course, after the course I had no fear or doubt about the move whatsoever. Additionally, in the two weeks following the UFC course, I gained five new coaching clients, even though it was almost Christmas, a time of year when people are manically busy and financially stretched. Two of these clients even paid for twelve months of coaching in advance! To me, it was a sign of what is possible when you back yourself in life. The Universe lends a helping hand!

Then amid all the excitement and joy, right in the middle of our packing to move to Sydney in January 2012, I received some news that impacted me greatly.

I Become an 'Orphan'

Just before I attended the UFC course, I had been running close to where I lived, in Caulfield Park, Melbourne, when I suddenly had an image of my mother come into my vision. I saw myself putting my arms around her and telling her that I forgave her for everything she had done in the past and that I wished her peace in her life and sent her love. I saw her crying tears of joy. Tears were also streaming down my face and I stopped running. Great sobs of relief poured out of me, relief to at last be free of any remaining resentment towards my mother. I felt shaken afterwards.

The next day, I related what had happened to Aleks, my friend and osteopath. Aleks listened and then said to me, "Christie. Your mother will die very soon. She has been waiting for this moment. Waiting for you to forgive her and send her love." Aleks, like myself, is a highly intuitive person, and in this moment, my intuition told me that this was going to happen, but to get on with my life until it did.

While I was travelling to the UFC course, I received news that my mother, who was living in Goa, had fallen down and been taken to hospital. I made arrangements for her to be cared for and discussed the possibility of travelling to Goa with my brother if she did not recover. As it was, she did recover. I thought that maybe I had misinterpreted the intuition about her being ready to pass on. I was happy that it was so. Since she seemed to have recovered, my brother and myself decided to go and visit her after my move to Sydney.

My mother had a further minor operation to aid her recovery from the one she had some weeks before, but had then slipped into a coma. Her condition started deteriorating and forty-eight hours later, she died. The doctors said that her passing was peaceful. It was as if she did not want to hang around any longer. Have you had an experience where you just knew something was going to happen, but had no logical reason for how or why you knew this? Then later things happened as you had expected? I was so thankful that I had sent my mother love before she passed away. Doing so aided the healing of deep past hurts for me. Hurts that had caused me to become fearful of life.

Experiencing The Healing Power of Love

One of the biggest factors that caused me to be so fearful in my younger life was the feeling that I was not loved by my parents. If children do not feel loved by their parents, they can start to experience fear. I had also learned to not love myself and therefore felt totally alone and defenceless. What I experienced on the UFC course had helped me to completely release any remnants of feelings of hurt, resentment and bitterness towards my parents, the 'Uncle' and the 'Nice' neighbour and replace them with feelings of love and appreciation.

It is said that the soul hangs around for a period of up to six weeks after someone has passed on. A week after the move to Sydney, I went to pick up Jade from the local school. The sun was shining down, warming my skin, the flowers a blaze of exotic hues, their fragrance filling my nostrils, and I could hear the cockatoos and rosellas noisily talking to each other in the trees. I felt an immense sense of gratitude welling up in me for being in such a beautiful moment, in such a beautiful place. Right then, I noticed something. I suddenly felt the presence of both my parents. I saw a vision of them laughing and happy together in a way they had not been while they were alive.

You will recall from Chapter 5 how as a child my favourite fantasy was that one day my real parents would come and find me. Now this vision of my mother and father made me realise that *these* were my real parents! How beautiful to know that my real parents did indeed come and find me! My eyes filled with tears of emotion and gratitude. My heart started to suddenly fill with love for my parents in a way I had never experienced before. I felt love for them, for myself and also felt the love they had for me. My body felt like it was expanding outward, growing to twice its size. This feeling of pure love was an incredibly important stage in my healing myself of the past.

From that point onwards, I noticed my appreciation of life increased to an even greater level. Has this happened to you, where a potentially sad event made you appreciate life more? I also experienced a profound sadness. The irony of my situation struck me with full force. Here I was helping people to feel good about themselves and create a life they love to live, yet I had not been able to help the two people in my life who needed it the most – my parents. I tried to assist my parents with their issues while they were alive as best as I could but I did not have the knowledge or experience I do now.

I now appreciate how much I learnt from them. It has been said that your greatest teachers are the people who push your buttons the most. They are the ones who force you to look at your reactions and emotions. When you react in a disempowered way, it shows you that this is where you need to do some work on yourself. As you have read, I definitely did a lot of work on myself thanks to my parents! What has been your relationship with your parents? What impact has this had on your life?

Following this event, a series of things started happening in my life that showed me very clearly that when you let go of the past, you create space for something new to enter your life. In Chapter 4, I described how I came across Akasha-Ka Meritamum and Sohial Fazram and the impact they both had on my journey to heal my back and my life. Some weeks later, the Universe lent another helping hand by sending someone else into my life who also assisted me on the journey.

Chapter 8: You Have Everything You Need To Back Yourself

The Potential 'Psychopath'

I was sitting at my laptop one evening after finishing my emails to my clients for the day, reading various Facebook posts. Up popped a friendly message from someone called Angelo Castiglione who I did not have as a 'Friend'. I did not know at the time that this innocuous message was to lead me to an amazing piece of knowledge and yet another powerful way of further helping my back to heal. Angelo asked me about the type of coaching I did. I wrote a brief description of the coaching and asked him what he did. So started a lengthy and fun written conversation. I learned from him about something I had never heard of before – the fascia, which I describe in the following section.

Angelo told me that he is a movement specialist and that since he had discovered myo-fascial release therapy, he had been able to help people who had physical issues turn their lives around. As you probably know by now this is a topic dear to my heart. I was fascinated, but also aware of being sold 'snake oil' – something that doesn't work. I wanted to know two things. Firstly, how on Earth does it help people? Secondly, could it perhaps help me with my journey to heal my back? So, I asked Angelo how I could find out more about what he did. He offered me a complimentary consultation and demonstration. I wished to return his kind offer, so I also offered him a complimentary coaching session. We agreed on a date and time for him to come over to where I lived so he could show me how myo-fascial release therapy worked.

After signing off Facebook, I had a temporary panic. It was brought on by the following thoughts. 'You don't know this person at all! He messaged you out of the blue. He is not connected to any of your "friends" on Facebook. He was super friendly. He offered to come around to your place way too easily. Either he is not busy so he is probably useless, or worse, he is a psychopath. Oh no!' I could feel my heart starting to beat faster. The thoughts continued. 'What have I done? I have invited a psychopath who preys on innocent women into my home. Help! I'll cancel the appointment. Too late! He knows where you live! Help!'

Then suddenly my Inner Power System cut through all the noise in my head. It asked, 'Do you really believe he is a psychopath? How did it feel when you were communicating with him? How does it feel now? Stop panicking. Go with your deepest feeling'. So, I stopped panicking. I went with my deepest feeling, which said, 'This is going to be amazing. You are in no danger. He is a lovely guy who wants to help others just like you do, just in a different way'. So, I went ahead with the appointment with Angelo, and the fact that I am writing this book shows that I survived! I will forever be grateful that I listened to that inner voice as it led me to another way of assisting my back to stay healthy.

A Little Known Part of Your Body That Does So Much

The fascia is pretty complex, but as this is not meant to be a book on human biology, I am providing you a simplified version of what it does so that you can gain an appreciation of how important it is in your body. The astounding thing about the fascia it that not only is it an extremely important part of the body in physical terms, but it also stores our emotions! Many years ago, the importance of the fascia in your body was not known. I learned from Angelo that the fascia was regarded as being a 'filler' and was often ignored and attention was given to studying more important things, like muscles, ligaments, tendons and bones. Then in recent years its immense importance became recognised and now millions of people including top athletes are benefitting from this knowledge but it has not yet become common knowledge. Have you ever heard of it?

Many people still do not know of the existence and the importance of the fascia. Yet knowing about the fascia and understanding its function is of benefit to millions of people in order to improve the quality of their lives on both a physical and emotional level. You are probably wondering why the fascia is not commonly known to people. There are many reasons, but the main one is that people are afraid of change. There have been a great many therapists and practitioners who have been reluctant to accept the new information regarding the importance of the fascia because it would lead to them having to revise their Model of the World. This sort of change makes people feel extremely uncomfortable as it then places them in new and unfamiliar territory, which makes them feel nervous.

So what is the fascia? The fascia is a tissue made of collagen, which is transparent and incredibly strong. If you took a chicken breast (apologies to the vegetarians and vegans reading this) and separated the skin from the meat you would see a thin membrane-like material that surrounds the meat and connects the meat and skin together. This is called fascia and it surrounds every muscle, organ, nerve and bone in your body. The fascia and muscles combined are referred to as the myo-fascial system. It also forms a large web in the whole body from your head to your feet, connecting everything together.

Poor posture, repetitive movements, inflammation and injury can cause the fascia to become tight and restricted. Apparently, the fascia holds emotions! Incredibly, emotional stress and events in your life can therefore also cause the fascia to become restricted. So, now you know why your body feels so tight and tense at times! When it becomes tight or restricted, the fascia exerts pressure on various parts of your body and soft tissue, which can cause pain and dysfunction. Parts of the body which are most commonly affected are the hips, thighs, arms, shoulders, back, neck and head.

Additionally, since the fascia is in one piece like a web, restriction or tightness in one area of your body can also spread to other areas of your body. For example, tightness in your shoulders can lead to a headache. Tightness in the fascia around your leg muscles can lead to your hips becoming tight. Some people can end up in a situation where the hips are so painful from the tightness that they are told they need a hip operation when really what they need is to relax the fascia. If parts of your arms become too tight from working out at the gym, this can cause tightness in your back. The fascia becoming restricted is what commonly leads to people being injured when exercising. If you feel stressed from having too much to do it can also cause the fascia to tighten throughout your whole body. Emotional upsets can cause a restriction in the fascia too, which will then make you feel tense and tired. The only way to relieve the tightness is to release the tension from your body. The great news is that this means you can also release some of the emotion stored in the fascia which is causing the tension!

I learned that in my case, the deterioration of my upper spine caused the fascia as well as muscles in my upper back to tighten. Additionally, whenever I was stressed the tightness in the fascia of my back became even worse. This tightness in my back then created a pressure upwards which also led to my neck becoming extremely tight. Yes. It was all interconnected and totally unpleasant! But help was at hand! Myo-fascial release is a manual technique carried out by many therapists where the soft tissue in your body is massaged or manipulated in order to stretch the fascia out again, which then restores balance back to your body regardless of what led to the tightness in the first place. If emotional turmoil or stress caused it you will also feel much calmer and more relaxed afterwards.

Rolling Myself to Even Better Health

Self Myo-fascial Release Therapy (SMRT) is a release technique you carry out on yourself using a round soft foam roller which looks something like a large cigar which is about 15cm in diameter and up to 90cm in length. My roller has a special design which has been patented by Angelo. It's called the MoveBetterRoller™ and it looks like a large blue cigar! You roll it on with different parts of your body such as your legs, arms, back and neck. Ideally, you start from your feet and work your way up to your neck so that you release the whole fascia as it is in one piece. Basically you use your own body weight to 'roll' on the roller massaging away the restrictions in the fascia yourself so that you do not always need to rely on therapists. You can do this anywhere at any time. Since you have already read how often I had therapy sessions in the past you will not be surprised to know how excited I was about this new discovery of SMRT!

From what I understand, doing SMRT improves your flexibility and performance and also reduces injuries. Another great benefit is that you can also release old emotions that have been stuck in your body for years. This is why I found it so super useful for myself. Not only was I helping my back and neck to stay flexible, but I was also able to release emotions that were stuck in my body and that had not already been released through my meditation, the courses I had done and the various techniques I used on myself over the years. Yes! We store a LOT of 'stuff' in our mind and body! We spend the first part of our life acquiring this 'stuff' and the later part of our life getting rid of it!

Since discovering the SMRT, I realised at yet another level that the body has the capability to heal itself. It just needs some assistance to 'wake up' to its own healing abilities. Adding the rolling to my regular exercise program increased the length of time between osteopath visits to between 6-8 weeks. With the combination of my daily meditation and the self-myo-fascial release (rolling) several times a week, my concentration and energy improved even further. This enabled me to create more tools and templates for my coaching clients than ever before. It also enabled me to start writing this book in parallel to the coaching. SMRT is a powerful way for anyone of any age to be able to help themselves both physically and emotionally.

Principle: You Have Everything You Need Inside You Already

I don't know how you feel, but for me it was tremendously exciting to learn about the fascia. It added another dimension to my belief that it is possible to heal yourself both emotionally and physically. It added further to the realisation that you and I are amazing beings! You already have all the resources you need to create what you most desire in life and lead a deeply fulfilling life. You have skills, talents, abilities and character. Your body has an enormous capability of healing itself. Your mind has neuroplasticity so is constantly changing, adapting and evolving. Neuroplasticity is also known as brain plasticity. It is your brain's ability to reorganise itself by forming new neural connections and altering existing ones throughout your life. This means that your brain is able to change and adapt based on your experiences in life and new information that you receive. We learn the most when we are children but really we can learn new things and create new habits at *any age*. My oldest client is in her seventies and in the process of creating a new life for herself. So, it is not just kids that can learn new things but adults too until the point they depart the planet! How fantastic is that?

This is a good point at which to reflect and to realise that you have everything you need inside you already. There is nothing missing! The thing that *is* missing is that you often do not recognise this and appreciate what you have inside you. Well, now is a great time to start!

Unleashing Exercise: Appreciating Yourself

This exercise is designed to help you look at what you already have inside yourself and what you have done with it. Take a piece of paper or a notebook and a pen. Write out the answers to all the following points.

1. Make a list of all your talents and skills.
2. Now make a list of all your greatest strengths.
3. Finally, make a list of all the things you have managed to do big and small in the last 12 months using these skills and strengths.

4. Thank yourself for being so awesome! This is a very important step.

It is always amazing to see how much you already have inside you and to see how much you have actually achieved in a short space of time but rarely recognise! Too often we focus on what we do not have and what we did not get done. Notice how you feel after doing this exercise. Yes, it's time for some self-appreciation!

It's incredible what we already have inside of us. The 'plastic' nature of our brain which enables us to keeping learning and adapting throughout our lives, the ability of our bodies to heal themselves, our gifts, our skills, our talents and our ability to love. Sometimes we are prevented from seeing how amazing we are because of the beliefs we have formed about ourselves. But it's time we started to love and appreciate all of who we are. It's time we stood in our personal power.

Chapter 9: Opposites: Back to Front, Front to Back

"There is nothing either good or bad but thinking makes it so."

William Shakespeare

Principle: Everything In Life Has An Opposite

For thousands of years, we have known about the fact that in nature and life everything has an opposite. Day and night. Cold and hot. Up and down. Left and right. This is deliberate in order to create balance. Think about it for a moment; if you have a plus and a minus and you add them together, what do you end up with? Zero. Neutrality and balance. If you only had one side, there would be a complete imbalance. In the same way, every event that occurs in our lives has both benefits and drawbacks, every trait we possess has both benefits and drawbacks and every situation we find ourselves in has both benefits and drawbacks.

The issue is that we are taught to only focus on one side of life and our nature. The so called 'positive' side. We are taught from an early age to focus on only our so called 'positive' traits and emotions and be ashamed of the so called 'negative' traits and emotions. How comfortable do you feel about being angry at times, or feeling impatient, or being self–focused? I am guessing that you feel this is somehow 'wrong'. This means that we are only accepting one half of ourselves and rejecting the other half. This causes the most enormous imbalance within us.

At times some of my clients have become anxious or depressed without knowing why due to trying to live just one side of themselves. For example, they felt they had to be cheerful, smiling and giving all the time, which caused them the most enormous amount of internal pressure. It is no wonder they ended up feeling anxious and depressed. Other clients have felt unworthy in some way, also without knowing why. They felt they ought to be driving themselves and achieving the whole time and felt frustrated with themselves, when they just wanted to take it easy or relax. When I helped them to accept both sides of themselves, they felt much freer and more balanced within themselves.

We are also taught that we should be happy all the time. This actually causes further imbalance within us and within our lives. We cannot be happy all the time. The law of nature says there has to be an opposite, so at times there will be sadness or unhappiness in some form. Instead of accepting this and embracing it we fight to be 'happy', which causes us an enormous amount of internal tension. I have lost count of the number of people whom I have met that put being happy all the time as one of their goals in life. When we accept being happy and sad equally, we experience a sense of balance within us, which feels very peaceful. Have you found yourself caught in the trap of trying to be happy all the time and then wondering what is wrong with you when you are not? Happiness is a transient emotion. It will last for a little while and then transform into another emotion. This is true of all emotions. None of them hang around forever. If they did it would be going against nature.

Opposites exist in nature and these opposites balance each other out perfectly. On a spiritual level, they bring order to the Universe. Below are some common opposites relating to our lives that balance each other out:

- Happiness and sadness
- Joy and sorrow
- Like and dislike
- Health and sickness
- Wealth and poverty
- Motion and rest

What are your thoughts regarding these opposites? I realised that my constant search for joy, happiness and pleasure was actually attracting sorrow, sadness and pain when I least expected it. When I started to accept both sides of life,

I also experienced fewer emotional ups and downs in my life. At some point a few years ago, I realised at a deeper level that opposites are indeed needed in order to create a more balanced life for myself.

When a particular event occurs, such as getting a promotion, we label it as a positive event and focus on the benefits it brings. However, we do not consider that there are also downsides to it such as potentially more pressure, longer hours and envious colleagues. If we are made redundant we call it a negative event and focus on the pain. We do not consider the potential upsides, such as the chance to find a new job with better pay and conditions. So many times I have seen it happen that people have found work with either better working conditions or pay or both or even started their own business as a result of losing their job!

The Glass Changes From Half Empty to Half Full

You will be familiar with the concept of there being two types of people in the world. Those who see the glass as being half empty and those that see it as being half full. My parents definitely saw the glass as being half empty. As a result, I grew up with the same mentality. This meant that if things didn't go the way I wanted in life, I would get depressed quite easily and sometimes even get into a total panic. This, of course, then caused tension in my body and more specifically affected my back and neck. My back and neck would become very stiff, causing me to feel tired and nauseous, which just made me feel even worse emotionally.

At these times, I would feel as if the world were collapsing in on me. This happened on a regular basis and I have no doubt that my reaction further affected the health of my spine and back. A horrible cycle to be stuck in. It obviously greatly affected the quality of my life. I often focused on the things that were 'not working' or were not the way I wanted them to be and ignored the things that were working or were the way I wanted them. How do you react when things are not the way you want them to be or things are not going as you wish? How does this make you feel?

Then I made a decision to try to change this. I learned a lot from the attitude of my brother Blaise. His view of the world was of the glass being half full. He would often focus on the aspects of his life that were working and as he wanted them to be and not put too much focus on the things that were not.

I noticed that this then gave him a consistently cheerful demeanour. I wanted that for myself! I realised that I had picked up the habit from my parents of often focusing on what I did not have rather than what I did have, what was not working rather than what was, and that this was dragging me down into a slight depression more often than was healthy.

My emotional state was constantly going from one of elation to one of depression on a regular basis. It was like being on a rollercoaster and I wanted to get off!! So I started to emulate my brother Blaise. I slowly started to put more of a focus on the things on my life that were as I wanted them to be and tried to be neutral or less reactive about things when they were not. However, it was a real struggle for me; my childhood programming went too deep. Still, I felt that there must be something out there that could help be break free from the prison I had created for myself, where I knew there was light in the world but I seemed to keep getting dragged forever back into darkness. Then one day, I did find the key to unlock my prison door when I did the NLP Practitioner course in late 2007 as I described in Chapter 8. The course helped me open the door and step out into a brand new world and set me on a whole new path in my life.

Transformation Through Knowledge and Insight

One of the key things I learned from the various courses I have attended and the research I have done over the years is that nothing has an inherent meaning except the one you give it. After learning this I started to realise that although I had viewed my childhood very negatively, in reality, if it had not been for my childhood, I would not have the level of knowledge I do now, or the level of life experience I do now. I had given the challenges of my childhood a negative meaning, but really they had provided me with a positive outcome.

The emotional pain I experienced led me to form a desire to heal myself. In turn, my desire to heal myself led me to gain a lot of knowledge that I was also able to use to help other people. This knowledge, in turn, gave my coaching added depth. Unbelievable! When I realised all of what I have described, I understood the law of opposites at a completely new level. I no longer understood it just in my head but deep in my heart and soul. Instead of my childhood being some sort of nightmare, it had actually been training that had helped to increase my knowledge and skills! There were hidden benefits which finally came to my attention years later! Now I am so grateful for everything the challenges taught me. How incredible is that?

This understanding was deepened after attending Unlocking the Freedom Code in 2011. The course helped me to take many events in my life that I had previously viewed as being unpleasant or traumatic and see with absolute clarity what they had actually taught me. This transformed former negative events into learning opportunities!

My understanding of the principle of everything having an opposite has helped me to dramatically change the way I think and react these days. As a result, I have completely transformed who I was many years ago and completely turned my life around. Even better than this, the principle has enabled me to help many others empower their lives through sharing this knowledge with them. What in your life still upsets you? What would happen if you could transform this?

Stirring It Up Exercise: The Opposites in Life

If you think about it:

1. Would you know what happiness is if you had not experienced sadness as well?
2. Would you appreciate harmony unless you also experienced disharmony?
3. What would happen if you were only in motion and doing things all the time? Would you appreciate health if you did not know what sickness was? Without being sick at some point how would you know you were healthy the rest of the time?
4. How could you appreciate pleasure if you had not experienced pain?
5. What would happen if you only gave all the time and never allowed yourself to receive? What would happen if you only liked everything?

Living the Opposites In Life

As I stated earlier we are taught to live one-sided lives and this means our lives are often not in balance. Additionally, when we are not truly embracing all sides of ourselves it causes an internal conflict within us. When I first came across this realisation, it was challenging for me to consider that what I had been taught and focused on for a large part of my life was not totally true. When I reviewed my life, I was distraught to find that for most of it I had caused myself a lot of anguish by believing that I should be happy, healthy, nice, bouncy, patient, etc. all the time. Although mentally I knew that you cannot be like this all the time, some part of me still somehow expected that I should and felt uneasy about the fact that I wasn't. Why did I feel like this? This came from my social conditioning. That is what other people around me were also doing.

When the veil that had been before my eyes fell away, revealing what was behind it was another life changing moment for me, showing me clearly the imbalance that still existed in my life. In that moment I gave myself permission to live both sides of life. To let myself be sad, flat, grouchy and self-centred at times. I had already been doing this for a number of years, but had often felt uneasy about it, as if I were doing something wrong. I made a decision to let go of the guilt and embrace all of me. I also gave myself permission to be sick at times without getting annoyed about it and accepted that at times there was going to be disharmony which, balanced out the fact that the rest of the time there is a lot of harmony in my life! What expectations do you have regarding yourself and your life? What impact does it have on you?

Since gaining the insights I have shared with you, it is as if some sort of weight I had carried for many years lifted from me. The strange thing is that I had not even been aware of the weight until it had gone! My body felt light and my spine seemed to extend a few centimetres, giving me the impression that I had become taller. I am only 150 centimetres in physical height, but I felt like my inner being had grown to 150 metres high!

I have shared the insights regarding opposites in life with many of my clients. The effect on them has been tremendous. The moment they realised that living both sides of life gives you balance, they started being much more aware of the way in which they are judging themselves and their lives and putting expectations on themselves to always behave in a certain way. They started giving themselves permission to be as they truly are. This put them on the path towards more self-acceptance and helped them to free more of their personal power.

One of my clients had been exhausting herself by trying to keep other people in her life happy. She had a busy job and was also looking to start her own business so she would work in the evenings or the weekends on building up the business. There were also family obligations where she was expected to go to certain family events and dinners and friends were asking for her help. All of this left her little time for herself and she found that she was becoming overwhelmed and drained.

She had been taught as she was growing up that you should give and not receive, because giving is more important than receiving. This one-sided focus was having a detrimental effect on her health and sense of well-being. I helped her to understand the importance of giving not just to others but also to herself. Additionally, allowing herself to receive was just as important as giving if she wished to remain healthy. She realised herself that based on what had been happening already, that if she did not, she would fall ill more frequently, have less energy and suffer mental anguish.

She made a decision to reduce the amount of family events she attended by half and to also not say 'Yes' to everyone who asked her to do something for them. She decided to only say 'Yes' if she had the time and energy. She also started to ask her partner to help her more often. As a result she stopped feeling so drained all the time and started to feel much more at peace within herself.

My Greatest Sources of Pain Transform Into My Greatest Teachers

One of the concepts I have been working on in recent years has been that of forgiveness, as I found this brings much peace into your life. In earlier chapters, I have shared with you the impact that forgiveness had on my life. However, I realise that every single experience I have had has taught me something valuable and forged my character. Without those experiences, I would not be where I am today. In view of this, I realised that my parents, my 'Uncle', the neighbour, had all indeed been my greatest teachers. As such, there is nothing to forgive.

This insight brought with it a feeling of love for them all as never before. I had already begun to experience love for my parents upon first moving to Sydney as I previously described in Chapter 8. Now, the feeling went even deeper and also included the two men who had been a source of pain for me in my early years. The feeling of love and gratitude was so strong that tears streamed down my face. My whole body felt expanded and a tremendous feeling of peace enveloped me. This latest insight was a culmination of all the other insights I had gained along my journey and which I have shared with you in this book.

To this day, I feel a deep sense of gratitude for everything they all taught me. As I have said before, they were my greatest teachers. Does that sound strange to you? Well, twenty or even ten years ago, if someone had said to me, "When you reach your forties, you will be grateful for all that you have experienced in your life, the insights and knowledge that you gained will enable you to enrich your life and the lives of hundreds of others," I would have assumed that person was taking some sort of drug which had severely affected their mental capacity. I would have replied, "You have got to be kidding! No way! These people ruined my childhood and my early adulthood. Why the hell would I be grateful to them?" It was so implausible.

However, it is precisely *because* of my past and the people in it that I can relate to so many people of all ages, both male and female. My youngest clients are in their teens, my oldest client is in her seventies and the majority are between thirty and sixty. When they speak to me about their addictions, I can listen without judgement and offer practical ways to help. When they reveal their sexual habits, I find there is nothing to be ashamed or guilty about. When they experience self-doubt and negative feelings, I can use the knowledge I have to help them feel better about themselves.

When they have rocky relationships at home or work I can help them find practical strategies to create harmony. When they struggle with their parenting I am able to reassure them and help them understand what is happening. Most of all, I can help them find out who they really are and to start to love and appreciate themselves much more. None of this would have been possible if I had not already walked down the path myself. My teachers are the people who led me down this path in the first place, and for that I will be eternally grateful to them. After all, they are the ones who taught me to learn to back myself in life!

Unleashing Exercise: The Power of Looking at Both Sides of Life

This exercise is designed to help you to increase your awareness that there are two sides to everything that is happening in your life. Here, the focus in on unpleasant or undesirable events in your life, as these are the ones that are most likely to cause you to feel unhappy and disempowered. In the English language, we use phrases such as, 'Every cloud has a silver lining' and 'Look on the bright side'. That is precisely what you are going to do in the following exercise.

Take a piece of paper or a notebook and a pen.

1. Write down as many events as you can remember in your life where an unhappy, unwanted, unpleasant or undesirable event turned out to be a blessing in disguise, i.e., something that turned out to be beneficial for you.
2. Now write down an event or something which was happening in your life recently that you were not too happy about.
3. How upset do you feel about this event?
4. Bearing in mind the principle of opposites, what might the possible benefits be from what happened? If you find it hard or have some resistance just 'pretend' that there were some benefits to what happened; you will be surprised at what you find!
5. Make a list of what those benefits might be. If you need ideas consider how this event might have benefitted you personally or professionally. E.g., it made me realise who my real friends are. It showed me how capable I am. The more examples you write, the better.
6. Check in with yourself. How strongly do you feel about this event now?

You will feel far less strongly about this event at the end of the exercise. Knowing about the opposites in life is immensely powerful in enhancing your experience of life and your acceptance of all sides of yourself. This principle has helped me tremendously, as you have read. It will do the same for you when you apply it to your life.

So far, I have covered the past with you and how I came to be where I am today and who I am today. In the next chapters, I cover where I am now and where I am headed in my personal journey.

Chapter 10: Back to the Present

"Happiness is not something you postpone for the future; it is something you design for the present."

JIM ROHN

Having shared my past history and learnings with you, this is an appropriate moment to share with you something that assists me continually in my endeavour to remain healthy physically, mentally and emotionally – the present moment. You have probably heard about living in the present moment many times, but are you actually doing it? My guess is that like most people many of your thoughts are about the past or the future. On one side, you find yourself thinking about what happened earlier in the day, or yesterday, the past week, month or even previous years. On the other side, you find yourself having thoughts about what is going to happen in the future, later today, tomorrow, next week, next month or in future years. When you are occupied with the past or future, where are you not? You are not in this very moment.

Think about it. When you have any issues in your life, where are they all stemming from? Your thoughts about what's happened in the past and your anticipation and expectations of the future. However, right in *this* very moment do you have a problem or issues? Usually not! You will remember from Chapter 1 that you have a strong connection between your mind and your body. So, when your mind perceives issues your body reacts, causing you to feel tense. Stress and tension lead to physical ailments. When your mind is in the present moment, it rarely perceives issues, and this causes the body to relax. Therefore, the more often you are able to focus on the present moment, the more relaxed your body will remain and the healthier you will be. The trick, of course, is learning how to let go of thoughts about the past and future.

Pain From Living in the Past

Many people I speak to reminisce on their childhood and wish they were children again with no cares or worries. You will know from the previous chapters that my childhood was not one that I like to dwell on and I have no desire to be a child again. The fear I had experienced as a child and the negative beliefs I had formed meant that I very rarely lived in the present moment. All of this affected my spine and back, causing my body to eat away at itself. Other people experience different physical ailments such as heart conditions, stomach issues, mobility issues and severe headaches.

It has been said that someone can only inflict pain on you at one moment in time. Any pain you continue experiencing from that event is self-inflicted. You are not letting go of the past and living in the present moment. The reason we do this is that we often do not get shown how to in our culture. The internal suffering I experienced for years as a result of my childhood was caused by not knowing how to move on from the past. At school, I learned math, English and many other subjects that were useful for my mind and helped me in a practical sense. What would have been invaluable though would have been to learn how to value and love myself, and how to let go of the past so I could live in the present. It was only in my forties that I learned how to do this.

In Chapter 6, I referred to the fact that my parents used to live in their past, which caused them a lot of suffering. Whenever someone commented on their behaviour, they would tell the story of what a hard time they had growing up, which caused them to behave like this. This was their excuse for not behaving appropriately decades later. Whenever my brother or I dared to comment that my mother's drunken abuse was unacceptable, her favourite phrase was "I have my problems." We could not see what problems existed in her life, so would ask her which problems she was referring to. Her response was the story over thirty years earlier of how her mother-in-law had treated her badly and how my father had done nothing about it. When we pointed out that this had occurred over thirty years ago, she insisted on hanging on to the story. She would then proceed to blame my father for putting her in that position and not throwing his mother out of the house.

Chapter 10: Back to the Present

My father's favourite story was how he had to start working at the age of sixteen and how no one felt sorry for him. When we tried to express how amazingly well he had done for himself now years later after such a challenging start, he would get annoyed with us. He did not wish to let go of his story. With both of my parents, our best option was to put some physical distance between themselves and us when they got into this misery mode about the past. Do you know people who insist on living in their past? What is it like being around them?

Looking back now, I can see that neither of them was willing to take responsibility for their lives. Living in the past and constantly keeping it alive is where they had learned to feel most comfortable. However, people fear change. No one was available to help my parents understand that by letting go of the past and all the associated bitterness and resentment they could change and have a much more fulfilling present and future. They believed that by continuing to talk about their challenging past, they would gain sympathy from other people. They were hoping they would gain love and admiration so that they could fill the empty hole that existed within them. When they discovered that what it actually did was push love and admiration further away, they became angry and frustrated. It was quite horrifying to observe.

In Chapter 9, I wrote about there being opposites to everything in life. You cannot have a drawback without there being some benefit at the same time. Although my parents' insistence on living in the past was a drawback for us, it brought some unexpected benefits for my brother and myself. Blaise and I learnt that we did not wish to live in the past. We learnt this watching the unnecessary pain my parents put themselves through. It greatly influenced us to appreciate what we had in our own lives. It also helped us to focus strongly on moving forward with our own lives. Another beautiful benefit we discovered is that by supporting each other through this challenging period in our lives, we formed a very close bond that remains to this day.

As I wrote previously, the irony for me is that I have helped so many people let go of their past and fill their emptiness with self-love but I was not able to help my parents, who were the most in need of this. Back then I did not have the knowledge or experience of life I do now. I feel such gratitude for what I learned from my parents as it has put me in a much better position to help others now. I could not give the love they needed back then, but it is never too late. I am able to send them love right now!

Living in The Past Destroys The Present

Even though I now realise the benefits my brother and I got from my parents, I previously did not know this. After living with them up until I was eighteen and then having them still involved in my life as an adult, I developed some fairly unhelpful programs within myself. This programming got in the way of me moving forward in my life and I found myself feeling like a victim of my past. I regularly felt sorry for myself. My internal story went something like this, 'My life is so tough! My parents did not show me much love; they abused me mentally, making me feel bad about myself. They did not protect me from being sexually abused as a child. I was laughed at in school because I developed way too early. I had few friends until I grew older. After such a tough life it is no wonder I do not have confidence in myself', and so on. Looking back now, I can hardly believe that this person in the story was me!

One day, I decided that I did not wish to be this way any longer. I will be forever grateful to my Inner Power System, which wanted to have a different story. It spoke to me very loudly and said, 'It is time to stop living in the past. Find ways to heal yourself of past hurts. Don't stop until you find what you need to help you create the type of future you want'. Thank goodness I listened!

Just by having this strong desire, I found that I was able to let go of the past to a degree just by deciding that I would. However, due to the intensity of some of the experiences I had, I was unable to completely let go of the impact the past events had on me. I explained in Chapter 8 that pathways in my brain had become 'locked' and kept me stuck in an old pattern. This showed up as Self-judgement, Self-doubt and my old friend Fear, as I have mentioned throughout this book. What patterns are you aware of within yourself? What would you be like without these patterns? The techniques I learned from the courses I have attended and the powerful knowledge I gained through all my research have helped me to start unlocking the blocks and finally free myself from the past, leaving me free to live in the present.

Principle: Live in the Present Moment

I am sure you do not need me to tell you that the past is over. It happened, but it no longer exists. We all know this, but sometimes we hold on to it. When we focus on a past moment or a future moment, we are not living fully. Why? Because we cannot live in the past or the future. We can only live in the present moment. This very moment is the only one we have. My thoughts often used to be about past issues and my expectations about the future, which then caused me to feel dissatisfied and unhappy. Many adults I know experience the same. Children live in the present moment. My daughter Jade has been my best teacher by showing me since her birth how to live in the present moment. When I observe her behaviour, it reminds me of what I have forgotten. Just by being herself, she is a wonderful reminder.

As children, we knew how to live in the present moment. More accurately, we did not know, we just lived like that totally, utterly, naturally. However, we learned to move away from our true nature. We were taught at an early age to live in the past or the future. This has resulted in us experiencing a certain dullness or flatness in periods of our life. At times we no longer feel fully alive. However, our brain has neuroplasticity and we can always change as long as we have the will to do so. We can teach ourselves to be like children again! We can learn to let go of the past and stop trying to live in the future.

This does not mean you do not have plans for the future or that you are unaware of what actions need to be taken in the future. It means that in this moment, you are not constantly thinking about these things and you are also not fretting or worrying about them. When you are living in the future, you are totally missing what is happening right now. Quite often, we have our focus on the next thing we have to do and we have not yet even finished what we are currently doing. One task is not yet finished and we are already focused on the next. Does this sound familiar to you? What effect does it have on you?

When I worked as a consultant there was a never ending list of tasks that needed to be done. Once I finished the things on the list, instead of acknowledging myself for having completed them and being present, I was already focused on getting on with the next set of actions to be taken. I was either in the middle of finishing one set of tasks or already busy fretting about the things I had to do next, which left my body in a constant state of alertness. There was rarely a time when I would let myself relax. If I did, I would somehow feel guilty, as if there was something else I should be doing. Does this happen to you? I was rarely in the present moment.

As you would expect, this constant state of being alert caused a lot of tension in my body that increased the level of stiffness in my back and neck, making them extremely uncomfortable at times. What impact does constantly being alert have on your body? When you live in the present moment, the mind and body start to relax. This means that you expend far less energy throughout the day, feel less tense and can end the day without feeling exhausted. Many people I come across would love to end the day without feeling drained and exhausted. One of the most powerful ways I know to do this is by staying in the present moment. For me personally, as I have learnt to live in the present moment, I found my body being able to relax more and my energy levels stayed pretty steady during the day. So much so that I could and still do coach clients late into the evening because I am not exhausted from my day. If you are not sure how to be in the present moment, the following exercise will help you to get started.

Stirring It Up Exercise: Experiencing the Present Moment

1. Notice how your body feels right now and what your thoughts are doing. On a scale of one to ten where one is pretty relaxed and ten is very tense what score would you give how your body feels right now?
2. Focus your eyes on an object in the room.
3. Start to notice the details of the object.
4. Now start to notice what you are sitting on or standing on feels like. Hard, soft, comfortable, uncomfortable.
5. Notice which parts of your body are touching the seat you are sitting on or the surface you are standing on.
6. Take three deep breaths in and out.
7. Notice how your body feels and what your thoughts are doing now. On a scale of one to ten where one is pretty relaxed and ten is very tense what score would you give how your body feels right now?

Your score at the end of this exercise should be lower than at the beginning, meaning that your body is more relaxed. There is only ever this moment. By living in the present you increase your level of well-being, rediscover the beauty of life and increase your sense of fulfilment. So when do you want to get started?

Chapter 10: Back to the Present

Unleashing Your Personal Power Through Being Present

We all hear about living in the present, but what does that entail on a day-to-day basis? The ultimate way of being present is called mindfulness. This is when you are completely conscious about what you are doing in each moment. For example, if you drink a glass of water, are you fully aware of doing so? I am guessing that most of the time you are doing it unconsciously. You drink the water and move on to the next task on your list, barely even noticing that you drank the water. Mindfulness means that you are aware of picking up the glass, of your movements as you pick up the glass and lift it to your mouth, aware of how the water feels in your mouth and in your throat as you proceed to drink it.

When you are being mindful in this way you are fully living in the present moment. This leaves no room in your mind for fear, negative thoughts or self-talk. Practising this in recent years has helped me immensely in my journey to backing myself in life by helping me to experience the tremendous joy that exists in each moment. It leaves no room for any negativity to creep in! It makes my Inner Power System far more accessible to me.

A lot of spiritual writing talks about living in the present moment. Think about it. All the issues we have are in thinking about what happened earlier in the day, yesterday, last week, last month or in previous years. Any anxieties we have are often based on what we have to do later on today, or tomorrow, or next week, or next month or in future years. But if we take this very moment right *now*, is there an issue? No. There very rarely is. The vast majority of the time people live in either the past or the future. This then robs them of the joy of being in the present moment where there is no issue. For many years, this was me. I was hardly enjoying the present because I was stuck in emotions from the past and worried about what the future would look like. Where are your thoughts most of the time?

Quite a while ago, I discovered how much of a strain it puts on my body when I am not living in the present moment. For many years my old friend Self-judgement would pull me into feeling bad about the past and my other old friends Fear and Self-doubt would pull me into panicking about the future. They got in the way of me backing myself with my plans. During these times, my body would react to my thoughts and start to tense up. This tension would not be released and over a period of days and weeks would build up and make the stiffness in my back and neck unbearable. However, at any given time, usually nothing of any significance was occurring.

Fortunately, the courses I did along with regular meditation, self-healing and self-observation all helped me to dissolve much of my dear old friends: Self-judgement, Self-doubt and Fear. I have shared with you earlier in the book the ways that I released and weakened these. Learning how to become present ensured that they stayed away. This remains true to this day.

The first way I started becoming present was by meditating daily. I found that doing meditation in the morning worked best for me and helped me start the day on the right note, feeling calm, centred and focused. Being in this state made it much harder to be pulled into the past or future as I was firmly in today! Still, as the day went on, if I had not managed to do everything I expected, I found that a certain amount of inner tension would build up. Some days in spite of my best efforts I started to feel overwhelmed and would almost become anxious. This led to me getting even less done. How ironic that whenever I got anxious about getting things done, I got even less done! Can you relate to this? This was obviously not the best strategy for backing my projects and being productive.

The problem was that not only did it stop me thinking clearly, but I also felt helpless. I felt as if life were happening to me rather than me being in the flow of life. How awful! It was clear that this was not a healthy way to be, but at the same time I could not just sit and meditate all day long. Then it occurred to me that maybe I could do some sort of meditation with my eyes open and walking around. Around this time I heard about the concept of mindfulness which I referred to earlier, where you are fully aware of what you are doing in each moment so you are fully present. I started reining my thoughts in from wherever they were in the past or future, and started bringing them back to what was happening right now. This worked very well for a while. Then I noticed that when my thoughts were particularly alarming or chaotic it was not so easy to rein them in. This is when I came across the book *The Power of Now* by Eckhart Tolle.

From the book, I discovered that by using your senses you can bring yourself back to the present. Notice what you are seeing in the surroundings, notice the sounds you are hearing, and using your sense of touch you feel your surroundings. It worked wonders! At first, of course, I had to remember to do it. I slowly started to practice it on a regular basis. Whenever I felt overwhelmed, I focused my attention on the objects in the room I was in, the surface I was sitting on or standing on and the temperature of the room. I became aware that this moment was the only reality. Everything else that I was thinking was a figment of my imagination. This simple act helped my system to calm down straight away. I was then able to think clearly. The interesting thing is that this then led me to getting through tasks with greater ease! Best of all, I maintained my personal power.

I am now able to be present in a way that I never was before. Many of my old issues from the past have been dissolved and others have been greatly reduced. This means that there is no strong pull towards the past and I do not worry about the future, leaving me free to be in the here and now. A number of my clients and my friends have commented to me that when they speak to me, they feel like I am fully listening to them. Of course I am! My mind is not full of 'chatter' about my own past or future. Through learning the art of how to be present my mind is not distracted and elsewhere. This is then where the magic occurs. Through being present and listening with my whole being I pick up a lot of signals from clients and friends which would otherwise be lost. Signals that give me an insight into what is really going on for them. I am then in a position to offer the appropriate assistance.

The wonderful thing for the people being listened to is that they then feel understood and validated. It helps them regain some of the power they feel they have lost or even 'discover' it in the first place! At the end of the conversation they feel uplifted and stronger within themselves. Who do you have in your life that you feel really listens to you? How do you feel towards this person? We often feel a bond or connection to someone who really listens to us. The wonderful thing about what I describe though is that it is not exclusive to me and the people in my life. It is available to anyone who learns how to fully live in the here and now. Their reward for being in the present moment is discovering pure magic in life!

Stirring It Up Exercise: Magic Through Mindfulness

Being aware of the way you move and the movements you make is a great way of being mindful. I got the idea for this exercise from Eckhart Tolle, who is a master on the topic of being in the Now! While doing this exercise, become fully aware of each movement you make. Give yourself permission to only do this right now. Before you start, notice how your body feels.

1. You want to pick up or inspect an object on the other side of the room where you are. This is your goal, so to speak.

    Your purpose right *now*, however, in order to reach the goal is to cross the room, being fully aware of the movements you make.

2. Start walking towards the object. As you do so notice the movement of your legs. How do they feel?

3. Stop once you reach the object and turn back. On the way back notice the movement of each part of your legs – your feet, your ankles, your knees, your thighs.

4. Start walking towards the object again and this time notice both the movement of your legs and also the surface that you are walking on.

5. Once you reach the object, turn back and on the way back notice your leg movements and the surface you are walking on again. Notice how your legs feel now as you walk and the feeling of the air on your skin.

6. When you are back at the starting point, notice how your whole body now feels.

7. Do the whole exercise one last time, luxuriating in the movement of your body and the feeling of the surface beneath your feet and the air on your skin.

The more attention you pay to the movements and sensations, the lighter your body will feel. When you pay attention to what you are doing, everything does indeed become easier and lighter. If you do not feel lighter perform the exercise a few more times. How many times do you walk to your destination hardly having even noticed what you were doing because your mind was elsewhere? When you do this the body feels agitated and tightens up. Being mindful in the way you did in the exercise helps you to keep your body relaxed and conserve energy. It also helps you to enjoy the present moment more. When you are in this state of being, you are able to access your personal power far more easily.

One of my clients teaches music in a school and is often having to walk to various parts of the building to teach as well as to attend meetings. At one stage, he had a lot to do and felt like he was always running around and it was making him feel tired and overloaded. I talked him through the mindfulness exercise above, and he felt the difference in his body immediately. He decided to use this technique as he walked from one appointment to another. After doing it for a number of weeks he reported back that he felt far less tired at the end of the day and also did not feel overloaded anymore. He felt much more in control of his day instead of his day controlling him. As you know, when you feel in control you also feel more powerful!

Another great way to stay in the present moment is to use the right questions to direct your thoughts away from ones that make you feel powerless to ones that make you feel powerful.

Principle: The Quality of Your Questions Determines the Quality of Your Life

Another of the key principles I learned from the NLP course I took and which helps me to this day is that asking the right questions is essential to getting the right answers. If you ask questions such as, "Why do you do that?" it can put people on the defensive and make them feel like they need to justify themselves. This of course does not make for a great relationship with anybody. On the other hand if you ask a question such as, "What makes you do that?" it is more of an enquiry and the person can respond without feeling the need to defend themselves. In the same way the questions we ask ourselves internally are immensely important.

I used to ask myself, "Why do you do that?" All this did was to make me feel frustrated about my own behaviour. "Why didn't my parents love me as much as my brother? Why did the neighbour abuse me? Why didn't my parents support me? Why, why, why, why?" It was maddening! It caused me to feel disempowered and worthless. It is no wonder I felt this way, as these types of questions cause your body and energy to contract. They cause you to lose the sense of your personal power.

To make things worse, I did not receive any helpful answers to my questions, but I did receive a lot of misery. After the NLP course, I started asking myself completely different questions such as, "What can I do differently? How can I help myself to feel good? What can I do to love myself more? How can I help myself to feel more confident? Which of the people in my life can I look to for support? " The energy behind these questions is far, far more expansive.

Asking myself these types of questions gave me very different answers, which helped me to free more of my personal power. I began to change my Model of the World to a far more positive one than I had before. Asking myself quality questions also helps me to stay in the present moment. Questions such as, "What do I wish to now?" "How else can I look at this?" "What might be the benefit in this?" prevent me from being dragged back into the past or forward into the future and help me to become present because I am considering what is happening in this very moment and the answer also relates to this moment.

One of the first things I do with my clients early on in the relationship is to get them to become aware of the type of questions they are asking themselves internally. Below is a simple exercise to help you get started in applying the principle in your life.

Unleashing Exercise: Empowering Yourself With Quality Questions

Take a piece of paper and a pen and draw a line down the middle of the paper.

1. Write down the types of questions you are asking yourself internally on the left hand side.
2. Notice how these questions make you feel. Are they empowering or disempowering you?
3. For each of these questions create a new question to replace it on the right hand side using the words What, How, Which and When.
4. Notice how you feel when you ask yourself these new questions.

Quality questions produce quality answers which help impart a sense of personal power. They are also useful for helping you to stay in the present moment. When you are preoccupied with the past or the future, it is not possible to sense your own power as it is covered over. By contrast, when you are in the present moment you get to experience the beauty of life right here, right now!

Who Has Got *Your* Back?

Chapter 11: Back to the Future

"The future depends on what you do today."

Mahatma Gandhi

We are often looking for ways to feel good about ourselves and our lives. In the following section I cover some simple things that you can do on a daily basis but which will have a big impact on your life now and in the future. You will probably not be surprised when you read about them. However, you will be surprised that they play such an important role in you backing yourself in life. Why is this? We often expect that we need to spend a lot of time, money and effort in order to enhance our daily lives. Something simple seems too obvious to be effective and…well, too simple!

In my experience I have found that it is often the simplest things that can provide us with a feel-good factor on a daily basis. Why is this important? When you feel good, you are able to back yourself more easily in life and also have a quiet sense of your own strength. Without feeling good you have a sense of powerlessness, which is not a good basis for creating a life you love. For much of my life, I searched for all sorts of ways to help myself feel good. As you have read, I invested a lot of time, money and effort and it has all definitely been worthwhile. However, all this effort was underpinned by some very basic life wisdoms which require little time, money and effort. Prepare to be amused!

Beware of People Selling Snake Oil

As you have read in the book so far, I engaged the services of many therapists until I found I could help myself to heal my back and greatly reduce the need for therapists. In my search to find a cure for my back I encountered a lot of 'snake oil'. Just in case you are not familiar with the concept, snake oil is a name for medicine you take which has no positive impact on you whatsoever. If there is any impact from it, it comes from the belief that it will help you. Your mind-body connection is so strong that by simply believing that something will be good for you it can have a positive impact on you.

Various people have tried to sell me 'snake oil' in the form of various supplements, health drinks and patches to be placed on the skin, promising that if I kept using the products for the rest of my life, I would definitely see some change in my condition. They contained anti-oxidants, vitamins and enzymes which can boost your health and assist your body. Some products even contained crystals. I gave each of these 'miracle' methods a proper shot over the years, one after the other, fully believing that they could rejuvenate and repair my back.

After some time I did indeed notice something different! Yes, I noticed my bank balance was getting lower paying the premium prices for these products. Unfortunately, my back felt exactly the same as it had always done prior to using these products. It is now obvious that they were in no way going to assist me in healing my back and my life as they never addressed the source of the issues. The principles that I have described in this book and the steps I have taken to heal myself are what helped me to heal my back.

I will state here that these products can be beneficial for your general health on a physical level, but that is not what was required in my particular circumstances. So I stopped using all of the 'miracle' products and substituted the following life wisdoms on a daily basis instead:

1. Drink plenty of water each and every day without fail. Your body is made up of between 50-75% of water, so if you don't drink enough, you 'wilt' just like a flower without water.
2. Eat plenty of fresh fruit and vegetables each and every day. It helps keep your cells healthy.

3. Get plenty of sleep. At least 7-8 hours. Your body repairs and renews itself while you are asleep.
4. Do what you love and love what you do. It gives you a natural lift daily!

As I stated earlier, these are simple things, but not always easy to do in modern life! If you constantly feel tired from not looking after your body and not getting enough sleep, as well as from any emotional issues you may be facing, it is hard to follow your dreams. If you spend the majority of your day doing things you don't love, your body starts to shut down. This in turn can reduce your energy and again make it difficult for you to create what you want in life.

For me, the four life wisdoms above are fundamentally important now and for the future. In my earlier life, I went to doctors at least twice a year. At the time of writing this book, it has been some five years since I went to a general practitioner (doctor) for anything. For me, that is proof that the four life wisdoms above work! When you don't look after your general health and well-being, it is harder to back yourself in life and to make your dreams and desires a reality.

No More Crack for Me!

In earlier chapters, I have mentioned the different types of therapies I have used over the years. It is appropriate at this point to give you some brief information about these therapies so that you have an understanding of what they entail in case you yourself wish to use any of them. When your body is misaligned or holds tension, it interferes with the flow of energy in your body and your ability to heal yourself. Releasing the tension frees your nervous system and enables you to achieve better healing.

Physiotherapists in general carry out treatment and rehabilitation of acute and chronic joint injuries. They also work on specific issues in your body. Chiropractors manipulate the vertebrae in order to bring the spine to a normal position when it is skewed, and also work with the underlying nerve structure in your body. Osteopaths take a holistic view of the patient. They take into account your lifestyle, work and leisure activities and diet. The body is treated as a whole unit. They carry out manipulation of the skeletal structure as well as gentle massage of the organs in the body in order to restore overall balance to your system.

Many treatment sessions I had with various therapists involved 'cracking' my spine or neck to release tension. This cracking often caused further issues in my body and I found that a few days after the treatments, all the tension in my back and neck would return. Apart from Aleks Hristov, none of the therapists showed me how to release tension myself from my body.

Network Chiropractors do not use any strong manipulation and are usually more facilitators. Earlier in the book, I described that they use gentle, specific touches to help your body release long-held tensions. The touches are intended to bring your brain's attention to the areas in your body that are holding tension, and encourage your body to release it. The Network method is much more aligned with where I am at now in my life. I wish to heal myself with minimal outside assistance, so this is what I have been turning to in recent times and is also what I intend to use in the future.

Principle: Energy Flows Where Attention Goes

Something else the NLP course taught me is that you attract the things that you focus your attention on. Whatever you give your attention to most of the time will grow or increase. According to this principle, if you focus your attention on what is not working in your life, then you will find that there are more things that do not work in your life. On the opposite side, if you focus your attention on what is working in your life you will attract more abundance in your life. Therefore, it is a much better use of your time and energy to focus on the things that matter to you and are working for you rather than what is not. If you want to manifest your dreams, desires and goals, focus your attention on making them a reality.

This principle shocked me when I first came across it. Why? Because in the past, I spent a lot of time focusing on what was not working in my life and what I didn't want. I was then dismayed and upset when the things I didn't want actually happened. For example, if I said, "I don't want this person to let me down," sure enough, that person would do something where I would feel let down. When I said, "I don't want to be late," for a particular appointment or meeting, I would end up being late. You would think I would have noticed that this pattern was occurring, but I didn't. Does this sound familiar to you?

After learning about this principle, I finally recognised what was happening so started to change my way of thinking to focus on what I *do* want. I started with saying on my way to appointments, "I wish to be there at the *perfect* time," and sure enough I started arriving at the scheduled time. On the odd occasions where I was running late, I noticed something very interesting happening. I found that the other people involved often arrived after I had or were only just ready for me. So I did indeed arrive at the *perfect* time!

I applied this to my back by saying, "I have a perfectly healthy and flexible back," instead of "I have problems with my back." It was a request to the Universe! This is when the Universe responded and some magic really started to happen in my life, as I described in earlier chapters. It is what led me to making the New Year's resolution to invest more time and effort into healing my own back, as I described in Chapter 3. This focus on what I wanted led to the amazing insights I gained as to how the earlier part of my life had caused the condition of my back.

Many times my coaching clients have said to me "I don't want xyz." I encourage them to turn it around to the opposite and express it in terms of what they do want. "I don't want to get stressed" becomes "I wish to remain calm." "I don't want my parents to bring me down when they visit" becomes "I want to have a great time with my parents." "I don't want to be in debt" becomes "I want to be financially abundant."

Time and again, my clients have reported back to me that they end up getting what they have focused on – the positively phrased things they have asked for, of course! Some examples are a more harmonious relationship with someone in their life, a more fulfilling and better paid job and more financial abundance.

Unleashing Exercise: Focusing on What You Want.

Take a piece of paper and a pen. Write down the answers to the following questions:

1. What are you telling yourself that you don't want? Write this down.
2. How does that make you feel?
3. Take out the word "don't" and ask yourself "What do I want instead?" Write out the answer.

By focusing on what you want, you create a different energy which will draw what you want to you, just like magic! By placing your attention on what you want rather than what you don't want, it will also help you feel happier and more fulfilled.

Freeing More of the Incredible Power Hidden Within Me!

One day not so long after I started writing this book, I was writing the section in Chapter 4 where I met Mike the Network Chiropractor at Prana House in Melbourne and was seeking to find a brief and easy to understand description of what Network Chiropractic is. It suddenly occurred to me that I had somehow not even thought to find a Network Chiropractor in Sydney. Instead, I had been using the services of osteopaths, albeit less and less frequently. After doing an Internet search I came across one name that seemed to have several entries - Euan McMillan. Wow! 'He must be good to come up in so many entries', I thought.

As I started to read his website, his words leapt out at me from the screen. I started to get the feeling that this person could be the right person to work with at this stage in my life so I called him to make an appointment. He advised me that the first appointment is an initial consultation that lasts around an hour to assess your condition and that the following appointments last between fifteen to thirty minutes. Having seen Mike at Prana House, I knew that this was standard so arranged the first consultation with Euan.

During the consultation, Euan did a 'mapping' of my back. On a diagram of the human back and spine, he drew marks in blue and red to show where the tensions were held. The blue marks were long-held tensions that had been there for years and the marks in red showed newer tensions which were due to physical day-to-day activities. You will not be surprised to hear that the blue marks showing the long-held tension were all in my spine! The red marks with the newer tension were more in the muscles of my back.

As you are aware, we store experiences within our body. In my case, much of the fear I experienced as a child was stored in my spine. This news about the tensions in my back was no surprise to me after the information I had received from Akasha-Ka and Sohial, as I described earlier in Chapter 4, in relation to how fear impacts the spine.

Using light touches, Euan brought my brain's attention to the areas deep in my body that were holding on to tension, then helped me to release it. These tensions could not be accessed using the foam roller I described in Chapter 8. My daily meditation helped to release a lot of the tension but I did not always know where to focus my attention. As I began to release the tensions, I felt a lot of emotions arise, which Euan reassured me was a totally normal part of the healing process. I found that as I released more of the tensions, my back and neck started feeling the best they have ever done. My concentration also started being even more consistent on a daily basis.

A Stunning Revelation

What was totally new for me was the revelation that the body does not always need to release trapped energy. Apparently, the body can reorganise itself and use the energy in a more helpful way. This put a completely new perspective on my efforts to heal myself. Up until now I had been focusing on releasing trapped energy and sending healing energy down my spine. It had never occurred to me that the energy in my body could also be redirected from one part of my body to another in order to heal myself. This was the most powerful insight I had received since I learned from Ben Harvey several years earlier that I could heal myself.

Usually during the treatments with Euan, every time he lightly touched some part of my body - my leg, or arm or a part of my back – that part of my body would start moving. For example, my leg would rise up in the air or move sideways. My back would start making movements up and down off the therapy table. Interestingly, even when I was not with Euan, I found that my body started to move of its own accord even when I was at home lying down on my bed or the sofa. So, I started asking the energy to move itself to where it could heal my body. I could feel it moving from one part of my body to another, which was followed by a feeling of peace. At long last - I had come home to myself! This resulted in my not needing another appointment for a long time.

Paying Attention Pays Off!

In November 2013, the top of my back and neck had started feeling pretty stiff again, so I decided to make an appointment with Euan. This is the first time I had ever gone nine whole weeks without some sort of therapeutic treatment!

As you can imagine, I was feeling pretty thrilled about it! Three days before the appointment after doing some meditation and then rolling using my foam roller, I realised that the stiffness in my back and neck was drastically reduced. The evening before the appointment, I also felt light and expanded. I was aware that I probably did not need the appointment and had a strong desire to cancel it. However, it was late in the evening and Euan's office was closed, so it was too late to cancel. There was also something else that made me want to keep the appointment anyway. I wanted closure.

The next day during the appointment, I experienced something for the very first time in my life during any therapeutic session. Pure laughter. In the past, I have found myself laughing briefly at times on a number of occasions during treatments. However, on this day, whenever Euan touched me lightly on my foot, leg, arm, back, neck or elsewhere, I found myself giggling and laughing like a child. Pure and carefree. It made Euan laugh, too. I knew in the core of my being that from then on, I would not be seeing him as regularly for treatments.

There was no sense of excitement, sadness, wonder or any other emotion. There was a completely neutral feeling. A sense of 'everything is just as it should be'. When we spoke afterwards, Euan told me that he found my energy was flowing freely and that there was a lightness and joy in me that he could feel. Of course there was! All the work I had done to heal myself over the years had brought me to this point.

From that moment on, I knew that in the future I no longer needed to rely so heavily on any therapists to assist me with continuing to heal my back. I have everything I need within me and more importantly, I know how to use it! This is why at times we struggle in life. We have the power within us already to create what we want in life, but we do not have the instruction manual that shows us how to use it. Our journey is to create our own instruction manual! I have shared parts of my instruction manual with you through my story, the key principles and the exercises in this book. In case you have not yet done the exercises in each chapter, I would highly recommend that you go back and do them. They may seem simple, but I can assure you that they are highly effective in triggering a change in the way you perceive yourself.

It gives me great joy to imagine you benefitting from the exercises and discovering even more principles for yourself as you write your own instruction manual. When you do it would be wonderful to have you share your experiences, ideas and comments with me! You can do that at the website for the book, www.whohasgotyourback.com, or on the Facebook page *Who Has Got Your Back?*

What Am I Doing Now?

Having read about my past and the key principles which helped me to heal my back and my life, you may be wondering what I am doing now. On a personal level, I intend to live to be well over a hundred years old. Therefore, I do a lot to look after my well-being and to continue my healing on a regular basis. After all, I only have this one vehicle (body) to carry me around, so I want to make sure that it runs smoothly until I depart the planet! To maintain it, I meditate daily and regularly visualise having a healthy back. I exercise and do rolling exercises on my foam roller several times a week. I drink plenty of water and eat lots of fresh food to nourish my body cells. Throughout each day, I focus on being in the present moment. I let myself feel that what I want is already mine. Not in some future moment, but right now. All of this assists in dramatically reducing tension in my body and keeping the energy flowing. I also laugh a lot!

Best of all, on a professional level, I do what I love every day. In Chapter 4, I wrote about the key stages in our development from newborn to adult. During these stages, as you have read, we form 'layers of life' that cover our true nature. You can also view these as being like veils that prevent you from seeing what an amazing being you truly are! Through my unique Self Mastery coaching program I aim to remove the layers or veils that prevent you from seeing how much you have inside you and how much you are capable of.

Using my own pain, life learnings and the knowledge gained from all the research and study I have done I am able to help my clients move rapidly forward in their lives. The principles and exercises contained within this book are a small sample of what I use to help people on the path to creating a life they love. My ultimate aim is to help people to become masters of themselves and their lives. Every time one of my clients removes a veil that clouds their view of themselves and they appreciate themselves more, it brings tears to my eyes and fills my heart with joy. In that magical moment, all the pain I experienced in my own life suddenly becomes worthwhile. I live for these moments!

In doing all of this, there is someone in my life who has had my back for the last seven years and whom I know I can rely on whenever I need. The lovely Martine Casagrande. Many times when I have been feeling low or feeling like I am struggling, Martine has offered her support. Sometimes, I have gratefully accepted it, but many times I have felt that I did not need to. By tapping in to my own Inner Power System, I have found all the strength I need. Nevertheless, it feels wonderful having such a special relationship in my life. As I mentioned at the start of this book, the idea for it came from a coaching conversation I had with Martine!

In the future, I intend to write more books in order to share more of what I have learned and to inspire people to connect with themselves and create a life they love.

I have shared with you the key stages in my changing my life from one that was full of pain to one that is full of joy and love. You will have realised that it was not one magical thing that helped me. It was a series of steps taken over years. With each step I took, I discovered more about who I really am and began to see myself more clearly. There is an old saying: "See yourself, free yourself, be yourself." When the veils of life are cast aside, you can see the real you, free yourself of your past conditioning and can be your true amazing self.

It is such an exciting journey to be on! The thing I love the most is that you do not need to pack or travel anywhere to embark on the journey. You just start from where you are right now!

Chapter 12: Backing Yourself

"Believe in yourself! Have faith in your abilities! Without a humble but reasonable confidence in your own powers you cannot be successful or happy."

Norman Vincent Peale

So far in this book, I have shared with you my personal journey to back myself in life and to heal my back at the same time. I have already shared with you some of the most powerful key principles and life wisdoms that have helped me along the way and which I felt would also assist you greatly with your own journey in backing yourself in life. In this chapter, I share with you some additional Universal life wisdoms that will add to the pleasure of your daily existence as well as empowering you in your life. You are probably familiar with these principles already. However, I find that although they are common knowledge they are rarely used or adopted by people. Why is this? Well, these wisdoms do not come with an instruction manual about *how* to apply them in your life given your personal circumstances! In this chapter I attempt to give you more of those missing instructions! Why is it so important that you apply these principles in your life? They will add a further dimension to freeing your personal power, which I am sure by now is not so hidden anymore!

Saying "Yes" Means Saying "No"

One of the ways I knew I didn't have my own back was saying "Yes" to various requests and then regretting it. My motivation in doing this was to please people so they would like me. If a colleague asked for help with a piece of work, I said "Yes", even though this meant that I had to work longer hours in order to get my own work done. If my manager asked me to do something, I agreed to do it without question and then felt overwhelmed by my workload. If a friend asked me for help, I replied with a "Yes", even though I was tired from all the long work hours and needed to relax. Do you do the same?

As you can imagine, all this extra activity resulted in my feeling tired and exacerbated the stiffness in my back and neck. Not only did I feel physically uncomfortable, I also felt emotionally drained at times. I know this is a common issue. Quite a number of people have expressed to me that they say "Yes" and then regret it. That saying "Yes" leaves them both physically and emotionally drained. So what is the solution? Realise that you are not a bad person if you do not say "Yes" to everything. When you put yourself and your well-being at the top of your priority list you will find that the ironic thing is you actually have more to give to other people because you are no longer drained.

The trick is to only say "Yes" if you have the energy to spare. If not, you can be polite but firm in turning the person down. If you are not ready to be direct, it is very useful to use delaying tactics so that you do not have to say "No", but also do not have to put an extra load on your depleted battery. Phrases such as "That is not going to work for me right now," "I have a lot on at the moment, so how about tomorrow/next week/next month?" "Of course I can…in a few days' time," are very useful. Of course, once you have your own back, you can also be much more direct. The additional benefit from doing this is that it will help you tap into your Inner Power System more and free up more of your personal power. The point is that by saying "Yes" to requests over and above what you are able to cope with you are actually saying "No" to yourself. "No" I am not worth putting first in my life. So next time you feel tempted to say "Yes" to someone else out of a feeling of obligation or need for them to like you, remember that you are actually saying "No" to someone else who is far more important – yourself!

Judging Yourself Is Not Having Your Own Back

Do you realise that when you judge yourself or use harsh words against yourself, you are showing lack of respect towards yourself? In that moment, you are not appreciating the tremendous value that you bring to the world just by existing. Part of your journey in life is to recognise the value that you add. The following example illustrates this.

Chapter 12: Backing Yourself

One of my clients felt that she was being attacked on all sides in her life. It seemed like her ex-partner, her parents and even some of her friends were against her. She came to me for coaching because she wanted to change this and to create something different for herself. Whenever someone seems to be under so much attack, I have found that it is because they often do not value themselves. My own past is a reflection of this. As you have read, I did not value myself when I was younger and therefore other people in my life did not either.

I asked my client how she communicated with herself. She told me that she was often saying these sorts of things to herself, "You only think about yourself," "You never get it right," "You don't deserve to be happy," "You are a bad person." It was as if I was listening to myself about twenty years ago. I helped her to understand that speaking to herself like this created a very strong energy around her like a magnetic field. This energy field was then attracting more harshness to her. This is why so many people in her life were also speaking to her in a harsh way. She was stunned.

Having realised what she was attracting, she immediately changed the way she spoke to herself. She also realised something else about what she was saying to herself. When I asked her "Whose voice is that speaking?" she realised that a lot of what she had been saying to herself had not even come from her. Her parents had told those things to her when she was younger and she had taken them on board. While she was growing up, her parents did not back her up, so as an adult, she was already programmed with the belief that she was a bad person and not worthy of feeling happy or feeling fulfilled. She felt she did not deserve it. She asked me, "But how do I know that it isn't my own voice?" I replied, "Your true voice would never speak to you like that".

Once I helped her to dissolve the belief about being unworthy and worked with her to increase her self-appreciation, she freed up more of her personal power. One step at a time, she started to take some big steps forward. She made some fundamental changes in her life. She sold a property she owned that was not covering its costs. The sale freed up extra cash each month, and she had a lump sum she was able to add to her savings and investments. She did not enjoy the job within the company where she worked, so she asked her manager for another role that she enjoyed far more. She also distanced herself from the people in her life who were causing her the most pain so that they were not constantly draining her. Some of her friends were so inspired by the change in her that they started asking her for advice regarding issues they were facing. She well and truly freed her hidden personal power! Once she started to back herself in life, she created pure magic for herself. Most importantly, she started to love herself for the first time in her life.

The Love Word

I have deliberately avoided plastering the word "Love" all over this book. When a word is overused, it loses some of its meaning and impact. However, it is my deepest belief that there is only love. Not just romantic love, but love in all its forms: Universal love. Everything else we experience is the absence of love. If we do not experience love we then experience its opposite – fear or other emotions driven by fear.

In her book *A Return to Love*, Marianne Williamson writes, "Love isn't material. It's energy… We experience it as kindness, giving, mercy, compassion, peace, joy, acceptance, non-judgement, joining, and intimacy. Fear is our shared loveless ness, our individual and collective hells… When fear is expressed, we recognise it as anger, abuse, disease, pain, greed, addiction, selfishness, obsession, corruption, violence, and war." Our inability to experience love is based on the conditioning we have received throughout our lives. This conditioning forms layers or veils that cover our true nature and prevent us from experiencing love.

When we start to back ourselves in life, we remove these layers or veils and can see the treasure that is hidden within us. Ultimately, there is only one job we have in life and that is to express all of who we are without hesitation or limitation. In freeing the hidden personal power within, you are already on the way to creating an amazing life for yourself.

Harnessing the Power of Intention

Intention is a powerful thing. When you set an intention it focuses your mind and energy on what you wish to create. Setting an intention before you attempt anything helps to organise your thoughts and helps your mind to relax. Why? Because when you set an intention your mind knows what you are going to be doing! When you don't set an intention your mind does not know what to focus on and your thoughts go all over the place, making you feel agitated.

An intention can be set for whatever you are doing right now, for the whole day, for the week or even further out into the future. An example of setting an intention for the thing you are doing right now is "I intend to pay full attention in this meeting." An example of an intention for a whole day would be 'enthusiastic energy'. This means that whatever you do during the day, you intend to approach it with enthusiasm and energy and whatever happens during the day, you intend to stay enthusiastic and energised! When your intentions are pure, you create more ease in your life. You will find that whenever you set an intention for anything, you gain a sense of calm. For example, setting the intention to have fun before doing a presentation can do wonders to soothe your nerves! When you know you have a very busy day ahead, setting the intention to 'Flow with the day' can also have a calming effect on your whole system.

You can set intentions for general things or specific things and you can set them for any area and level of your life: mental, emotional, physical, social, financial, work, business, spiritual, etc. The key thing to note here is that by setting an intention you are actually calling on Universal energy to help make it happen. This is when amazing things start to occur in your day and life.

Unleashing Exercise: Setting Daily Intentions

It is always helpful to start the day on a positive note. A lovely way to do this is to have some positive intentions for yourself. They do not need to be particularly clever or complicated; the only requirement is that you feel good about the intentions you set for yourself. They have to resonate with you. Below are some examples to get you started but over time you will start creating your own. You can start on any day of the week and pick one intention for the whole week or try a different one each day.

Day 1: I Go With The Flow Of Life

Day 2: I Am Fully Supported By The Universe

Day 3: Everything I Need Is Already Within Me

Day 4: Life Is Full of Possibilities

Day 5: I Am Growing and Expanding Daily

Day 6: I Am Open To New Ideas

Day 7: I Am Worthy Of Love

Set the intention before you go to sleep at night and again when you wake up first thing in the morning. I also put mine in my calendar system as a reminder to me throughout my day of my intention. You could do the same or write it on a piece of paper or an index card and carry it around with you in your pocket or handbag as a reminder. Set the intention and notice what happens during your day when you stick with it! A number of the intentions above have been created to allow you to be kind to yourself. Being kind to yourself is powerful medicine in your life and it is the last principle I am introducing in this book.

Principle: Communicate With Yourself With Kindness

This last principle is the one that underpins all the other principles in this book. It is at the heart of all the exercises in the chapters. For me, it is the one that makes my heart sad when I remember all the times in my life when I have not been kind to myself. All the times I have said harsh things to myself. All the times I have tolerated unreasonable behaviour from other people. All the times I have said "Yes" when I really wanted to say "No". All the times I have tried to please other people. In all these times I was being unkind to myself.

When we do not back ourselves in life, we communicate with ourselves harshly. We criticise ourselves. We are impatient with ourselves. We judge ourselves. We do not show ourselves appreciation. We expect a lot from ourselves and are disappointed when we do not live up to our own expectations. We try to please others and then feel awful when we don't manage to do it. None of this shows kindness towards our own selves. If that was our best friend, we would never dream of communicating with him or her in that way. We would be much more understanding, patient, supportive and kind.

By communicating with yourself with kindness, it introduces a new energy into your life. An energy of self-appreciation and self-love. There's the "Love" word again! What follows is a final, fun (well, I find it fun!) exercise for you to do in order to help you bring this wonderful new energy into your life. It enables you to tap into your Inner Power System more.

I have based this last exercise on a list that Ben Harvey got me to write during the time he was mentoring me. Some people do a similar exercise by looking into their own eyes in a mirror and saying what they appreciate about themselves out loud and then ending it with "I love you" or simply saying "I love you" every time they see themselves in any sort of mirror. It is a great exercise but for it to work in creating more self-love and appreciation it needs to be done on a daily basis. I have found that looking in a mirror and speaking to yourself feels very awkward for people, so they are likely to abandon the exercise fairly quickly. I therefore prefer Ben's version because even though it can still be a challenge for some people it is far less awkward than looking in a mirror!

Unleashing Exercise: Fifty Things I "Lurve" About Myself

Take a piece of paper or a notebook and a pen.

1. Write a list of fifty things you love or "lurve" about yourself.

You may be wondering why I use the word "lurve". You are right, it is not a real word. It is a psychological trick! The word "love" carries a big charge for some people and some clients I have given the exercise to have felt awkward about using the word "love" because they have learnt to judge themselves harshly. I found that using a nonsense word takes the charge out and enables them to carry out the exercise successfully.

Anything is valid as this list is for you and you only. There is absolutely no need to try to impress anyone else. So go ahead and show yourself some appreciation!

For example:

I love the way I brush my teeth.

I love that I am a good friend.

I love that I can get dressed by myself.

I love the way I lick my plate clean after eating. (Well, this doesn't have to be such a serious exercise. You are allowed to have fun with it!)

The result from doing this exercise is that you start to form a deeper relationship with yourself.

2. Read the list to yourself every morning and before going to bed.

I recommend to my clients that they make a copy of the list and have one at home and one at work, and you will also find this helpful. Every time your mind tries to draw you into self-criticism, it is a great way to bring you back to a place of self-love.

Rewiring Your Brain

You will have noticed that I place a lot of emphasis on writing things down. Nearly all the exercises in this book involve writing. You may be wondering why I am doing this unless you already know the answer! I have found from research that the most effective way to retain anything new you have learned is to write it out by hand. Writing something down on paper stimulates something called the Reticular Activating System (RAS), which sits at the base of your brain. The RAS is, in simple terms, a collection of cells which filter all the information that your brain receives and give more attention to what you are currently focusing on. Apparently the physical act of writing brings the information that you are writing to the forefront of your brain and triggers you to pay close attention to it and therefore retain it.

You will have also found that some of the exercises require you to write lists. Whenever you write a list, new neural connections form in your brain. The more you write, the stronger the neural connection becomes, enabling you to develop new ways of thinking. Typing things up does not work as effectively.

What Does Having Your Back Look Like?

In Chapter 1, I wrote that having your own back does not mean that you cannot turn to other people and ask for assistance when required. But there is a big difference between asking for help to make life easier and being totally dependent or leaning heavily on other people for support because you feel you cannot rely on yourself. I liken this to using other people as a crutch to prop you up versus having someone hand you a crutch so you can prop yourself up. When you have your own back it means you feel able to trust your own judgement. Able to trust yourself to do what is right for your life. Able to rely on yourself to get things done. Able to make more use of your Inner Power System for guidance.

It also means accepting all your traits, both good and bad, without judgement. This is appreciation of yourself and the amazing being that you are. Appreciation of all that you have already created in your life and all that you will be able to create in the future. All of this though is my personal view of what 'having your back' looks like. What is your view of it? This is really the most important and relevant view as it is what is going to drive you forward in creating a life you love!

In Chapter 1, there is an Unleashing Exercise: How Strongly Do You Have Your Back? Can you recall how strongly you seemed to have your back at the time of doing the exercise? Since then you have learned about some key principles and done further exercises in order to help you apply these in your life. If you go back and do the exercise In Chapter 1, you will find that your answers are now different to what they were originally. How strongly do you back yourself now? What have you learned about yourself? What do you now appreciate about yourself? How often are you now aware of your personal power? When you are able to love and appreciate yourself, it connects you much more strongly with your own personal power. Once you have this connection, it will never leave you. No matter what is happening in your life, no matter how many ups and downs you experience, you will find the strength to deal with them. When you are aware of just how much treasure lies within you there is no limit to what you can achieve in your life. Isn't it time you started to live a life you love?

Who Has Got *Your* Back?

Conclusion

Throughout this book, I have shared with you the Universal wisdoms of life and the key principles that have helped me on the journey to healing my back and healing my life. You have seen that healing myself of past hurts and backing myself in life has had the biggest impact on the healing of my physical back. It is an ongoing journey. My deepest desire in sharing the journey with you is that you apply the principles in your own life so that you remove your own blocks on the way to creating a life you love.

It is wonderful to have people in your life who have your back. It helps you to feel supported, connected and loved. The biggest gift you can give yourself, however, is to feel such a deep connection with yourself, such gratitude for being who you are and such a profound appreciation of how amazing you are, that you do not need to rely on anybody else to have your back. You have yourself, now and forever.

When I first decided to write this book, the idea was to share with you the story of how I started to heal my back and use the story to show you that it is possible to heal yourself and to inspire you to do so using the principles that have helped me a great deal. The exercises contained within the chapters are deceptively simple, but there is power contained within them. When you complete the exercises you will discover that they provide you with insights into yourself and strengthen your ability to back yourself in life.

Do not be afraid to seek help when you need it. I would not have progressed as rapidly and effectively in my own journey if I had not sought the knowledge and wisdom of other people. As you have read, I did not allow myself to become dependent on any of these people, instead choosing to consult them in order to gain ideas or knowledge and then helping myself as much as possible. In a similar way, the clients who engage my services are not reliant on me to back them. They back themselves in their own lives and use my knowledge and experience to help them move past their blocks and create what they want in life much faster. Backing yourself in life and choosing to enlist the assistance of others when required creates a sense of empowerment.

Once you start applying the principles I have shared with you in your life, they begin to uncover the treasure which is often hidden from you, covered over by layer upon layer of life events. The principles are key to removing these layers and rediscovering that quiet power that is inside you. Your ability to access your personal power is essential to you being able to back yourself in life and take action to make your dreams and deepest desires come true. Many people go through life not backing themselves and therefore not achieving their dreams. I have met some people who have given up on their dreams and resigned themselves to a life of mediocrity and only feeling half alive. Just by you reading this book it is clear that you are not one of these people!

Over a decade ago, the prognosis I received about the condition of my back was that by now parts of my spine would most likely have fused together, I would have less flexibility in my spine, would feel pretty uncomfortable and would need frequent treatments from a physiotherapist, chiropractor or osteopath in order to alleviate the symptoms. I am happy to report that none of this has come about.

No parts of my spine have yet fused together. The stiffness in my back and neck is enormously reduced. The dizziness and nausea I used to experience are a distant memory. My ability to concentrate is far more consistent. My back is now more flexible than when I was younger and I am expecting that as I age my back will remain flexible, supple and strong. It is no longer a remote hope or possibility. It is a reality that I have already created for myself through my total commitment to my well-being. In the end it always was, is and will be down to me to work with the Universe to create what I want for myself in life. The same is true for you. Nobody else can do it for you.

It is my intention to remain aware of everything I already have within me and to use the gifts I have been given to help as many people as possible transform their lives before I depart the planet. I see the principles that are contained within this book as a stepping stone in your life journey. I know you will be seeking out many other principles to back yourself ever more strongly in life and to uncover even more of your own personal power.

My greatest desire is that one day we will meet. Maybe in the street, or your favourite café, or a beautiful park. We will somehow recognise each other. When I ask you, "Who has got your back?" you will look me straight in the eyes with a smile playing on your lips and reply, "I have, Christie. I have. I am the only one who can."

Resources

Education, continuous learning and ongoing coaching or mentoring are essential for anyone wishing to truly free their personal power and fully back themselves in life.

Mentors

All of these outstanding mentors run seminars, programs and workshops in Australia and throughout the world.

Paul Dunn: www.pauldunnonline.com

Benjamin J. Harvey: www.benjaminharvey.com

Martine Casagrande: www.livinglovingit.com.au

Emily Gowor: www.emilygowor.com

Bibliography and Suggested Reading

A Return to Love, Marianne Williamson

The Power of Now, Eckhart Tolle

You Can Heal Your Life, Louise Hay

The Power of Intention, Wayne Dyer

The Four Agreements, Don Miguel Ruiz

Acknowledgments

There have been so many people that have helped me on my journey in healing my back and life that it is hard to know where to start. Everyone I have ever had contact with has touched my life in some way either directly or indirectly.

Most importantly, my first thanks go to my brother Blaise. As children, we both fought and helped each other! We were able to support each other through some of the toughest times with our parents which created a deep bond between us. As we grew older, Blaise was one of my biggest fans and a tower of strength and support in some of my lowest moments. The bond between us remains as strong as ever and despite the thousands of kilometres between us in physical distance, I always carry him in my heart. There are no words that can adequately express my gratitude to you Blaisey, so I will say a simple "Thank-you" multiplied by a thousand times! Love you forever, my dearest brother.

My gratitude and respect goes to Benjamin J. Harvey who came into my life at just the right moment! I attribute the early success of my coaching business and my moving further along the path towards healing my back to his guidance. His love and his willingness to share his profound wisdom with me have made a lasting impression on me. Ben you rock!

My deepest gratitude goes to my friend and soul sister Martine Casagrande. Where would I be without her? Since we met, we have learned an incredible amount from each other. She has been (and still is) a constant source of wisdom and strength for me when I need it. I love that I am able to play a similar part in her life. I have never had a relationship like this with anyone. Over the years, she has inspired me to back myself ever more strongly in life and to also write this book and for that I will be forever grateful. My heartfelt thanks go out to you Martine for your unending love and support. Love you, darling.

When you want to get to where you want to go faster, you need a coach and mentor. Emily Gowor has been an unbelievable source of support for me in writing this book. Emily used her magic to help me turn a myriad of disparate lifetime experiences and knowledge into a coherent whole! Without her, this book would have been a messy bunch of ideas and published in another two years' time. Being my first book it was wonderful to be able to call upon Emily's wisdom and experience in book writing. I want to thank you, Em, from the deepest part of my heart for the love and support you have given me in so many ways since we started our journey together. Here's to more soul-searching and fun times together!

Much gratitude and respect goes out to Euan McMillan, Aleksandra Hristov and Mike Melling-Williams for their generosity in sharing their knowledge and wisdom with me. Their skills and loving care of their clients make them truly stand out from so many other therapists I have worked with. Special thanks go to Akasha-Ka Meritamum and Sohial Fazam, whose valuable insights were the catalyst for writing this book. The world needs more people like you!

To all my clients over the years, thank you for allowing me to learn and grow with you. The beauty of my life and the depth of my wisdom have grown from all the insightful hours spent with you. It has been a privilege to witness you backing yourselves ever more strongly and transforming your lives.

My warmest gratitude goes to my gorgeous husband Eiko and my beautiful daughter Jade for enabling me to do what I do and still have a home life! A big thank-you for your patience with me in my grumpy and self-centred moments and celebrating my highlights with me. There are many more fun years to come. Love you both so much!

Last but not least, a big thank-you to myself for listening to my Inner Power System for so many years even when it made no logical sense. I truly appreciate my persistence and commitment to myself even when the going has been tough. My willingness to believe in myself has brought me to this point and what an amazing journey is has been so far. I am looking forward to even more adventures in the future!

Much love and light to each and every one of you.

About The Author

Christie Pinto is a dynamic Personal Coach, Mentor, Healer and Author. Christie's vision is to help millions of people around the world connect with themselves so they can live life on purpose and create a life they love while having a lot of fun.

Within the last decade, Christie has already assisted many people around the world to lead more purposeful and fulfilling lives. Regarded by many as an inspiration, Christie is the author of *Who Has Got Your Back?* and owner of Crystal Clear Horizons, a company dedicated to delivering cutting edge coaching, mentoring and training to people who want to enjoy life and make a difference in the world.

With a corporate background in information technology and projects, Christie found that after more than fifteen years in this arena, her true purpose lay elsewhere. At the age of forty, Christie made the courageous decision to follow her heart, moving into the coaching space. Her background as a senior consultant enabled Christie to combine her new coaching and healing skills with business knowledge to deliver a holistic approach. She draws deeply on her professional and personal background to impart insights and wisdom to her clients and audiences.

One of Christie's outstanding talents is the ability to seamlessly combine her knowledge of Universal Laws, NLP, coaching and business into a whole. She refers to what she does as 'combining the spiritual with the practical': "I love it when my clients start to see the bigger picture of life from a higher perspective and their issues at a daily level suddenly become insignificant or disappear altogether."

In order to take inspired action people need access to material in a format that suits them. With this foremost in mind, Christie divides her time between coaching people who want to make a difference in the world, writing, self-development programs and multimedia work.

Would You Love to Lead a More Fulfilling Life?

Hi there!

I meet many people who are not living the way they really want to and often feel like something is missing. They are not enjoying their work or their business, or are struggling with personal or work relationships. Quite a number suffer from confidence, self-esteem and self-worth issues, and have been for years. Many of them need guidance to get them to where they want to go much faster.

My company, Crystal Clear Horizons, is dedicated to helping people who want to live a deeply fulfilling life and make a difference in the world. Our mission is to inspire millions of people worldwide to connect with themselves so they can live life on purpose and create a life they love while having a lot of fun.

With this in mind, we are thrilled to offer you The Self Mastery Program. This unique personal coaching and mentoring program is completely tailored to your individual needs and circumstances. Wherever you are in the world, we come to you!

The program is delivered in three impactful stages.

1. **Stage 1: SELF AWARENESS**

    You attain deep insights into how you got to where you are and create absolute clarity on where you want to go.

2. **Stage 2: BUILD LIFE SKILLS**

    You boost your skills with tools and techniques that help you to easily dissolve your issues and accelerate towards your dreams and desires.

3. **Stage 3: SELF MASTERY**

    This is the really fun part! You feel inspired to create the results you most desire in life. You have a deep sense of purpose and are crystal clear on your future life direction. Most importantly, you feel like the master of yourself and your own destiny.

I invite you to back yourself and make today the day you start to live a life that you love!

You can find the full details of the Self-Mastery Program at:

www.crystalclearhorizons.biz

Yours in inspiration,

Christie Pinto

Founder of Crystal Clear Horizons

www.ingramcontent.com/pod-product-compliance
Ingram Content Group UK Ltd.
Pitfield, Milton Keynes, MK11 3LW, UK
UKHW021313180426
11947UKWH00015B/1193